FRETBOARD: FOR BEGINNERS

2 Manuscripts in 1 Book, Including: How to Play Guitar and How to Play Ukulele

Preston Hoffman

Table of Contents

HOW TO PLAY
GUITAR
IN 1 DAY
The Only 7 Exercises You Need to
Learn Guitar Chords, Guitar Scales
and Guitar Tabs Today
PRESTON HOFFMAN

BOOK 1

HOW TO PLAY GUITAR: IN 1 DAY

The Only 7 Exercises You Need to Learn Guitar Chords, Guitar Scales and Guitar Tabs Today

Preston Hoffman

Table of Contents

Introduction

Thank you for purchasing this book. You are now already on your way to becoming a guitarist.

The guitar is one of the most versatile instruments that there is and one of the most straightforward to play. Becoming a player opens you to a world of fun, relaxation and satisfaction.

For some, it might lead to a bit of extra income, if you join a band. Making music is a wonderful thing; making it in the company of others is even better.

By buying this book, you have made the first move to acquiring lifelong skills, which will provide much laughter, much joy and immense satisfaction.

We suggest that you work through this book a chapter at a time, spending long enough in each lesson to have secured the skills before moving on to the next chapter. It may seem hard at the outset, but it will quickly become easier.

This is a very practical book. You will be playing straight away. There are two useful chapters at the end, which offer more detail on questions that might arise, and a glossary of terms. There are also some songs to get you playing.

Mostly, this book will introduce you to playing the guitar. Give yourself a day, and you will be well on your way.

Chapter One: Getting Started – Lesson One - The Parts of the Guitar, and How to Hold It

The saying goes that there is no time like the present, so if your aim is to learn to play the guitar quickly, let us get straight into it.

Essential Information

A few notes, though, before we start. There is a glossary at the back of this book. Any term followed by an asterisk (*) will be defined in the alphabetical glossary at the end.

Secondly, a very useful tip is to get your head around each chapter before moving on to the next. The better understanding you have of each section, the more rapid your progress will be.

In addition, the learning will stick, and you will not have to constantly look back to re-learn the skills that this book will help you to acquire.

Next, don't worry if you get sore fingers on your left (fret*) hand, especially if you are playing a steel string guitar. The skin on the end of your fingers will quickly harden and the soreness will disappear.

OK, let's get on with it. For the purposes of the rest of the chapter, the assumption is made that you already have your guitar, and that it is stringed and tuned*. If not, there are sections on choosing your guitar, stringing it and tuning the instrument later in the book.

The Parts of the Guitar

The guitar is formed from a few basic parts, each of which has their individual role. It doesn't really matter which kind of guitar you own, because the make-up is the same. If you have an electric guitar, there will be extra knobs and levers, but we will look at these later.

Guitar Head and Tuning Pegs

The head has two primary purposes. It is there to help sustain, or lengthen, the sound of the strings.

If you put your hand on the head, and play the open* strings with the other hand, you will sense the vibrations of the notes continuing to make a sound.

The second role of the head is hold the tuning pegs. These are the pegs connected to the rollers around which the strings are held tight. Turning these pegs changes the note. See the section on 'tuning' for more details.

Heads look different on the various types of guitar; do not worry about this, as they all perform the same task.

Guitar Neck and Nut

The picture above shows the nut. This is the part of the that holds the strings in place.

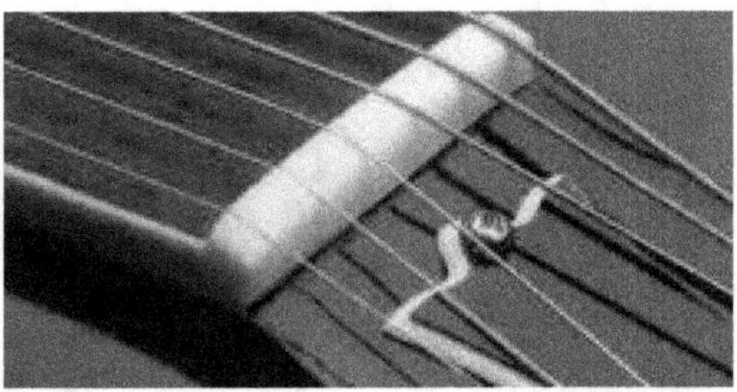

The nut has six little slots into each of which a string fits. It ensures that a full sound is heard by keeping the string away from the neck and frets.

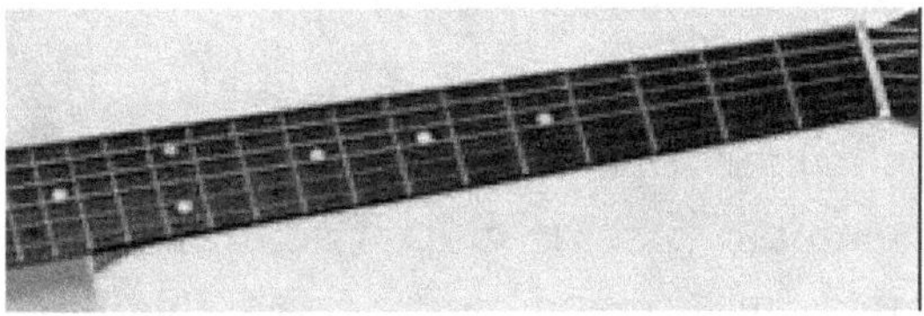

The picture above shows the neck of a guitar. This is the long section on which the frets are located. The example above has fret markers – the little dots that help the player to locate the appropriate fret when playing down the neck, which is more difficult than playing up at the head end. Not all guitars have these markers.

Here we can see the body of the guitar. The hole in the middle is called the sound hole, which is there to amplify the sound of the guitar. Electric guitars do not have these, as they have pick-ups (raised metal bars) to send the vibrations electronically to the amplifier.

Note that the body shape of a guitar can take many forms, especially with electric guitars. The final part of the guitar to identify is the bridge, into which the ends of the strings are fitted.

Holding the Guitar

As a beginner, it is best to start with a sitting position. As players become more experienced, then it is possible to play standing up, but the extra support offered when sitting helps the new player.

The position above is the classical stance when playing the Spanish* guitar. Note that the left foot is raised. A footrest can be purchased to facilitate this, but a pile of books or a block of wood works just as well. The guitar sits on the left leg, with the right just offering support. Both hands then fit into the natural position.

For larger guitars, such as acoustics*, then the picture below offers a more usual position. Here, the guitar is on the right leg, with the two legs close together. Of the two, the better one for the beginner is the Spanish guitar position. However, comfort is the most important thing of all.

Chapter Summary

So now we have the basics.

- You know the names of the parts of the guitar
- You know how to hold the instrument

In the next chapter you will begin to learn how to play.

Chapter Two: Lesson Two - Chords

In this chapter we will learn about the basic chords* which will allow you to begin to play songs almost immediately.

For a right-handed person, or somebody who plays right handed (most people do…) chords are formed with the left hand. Many songs can be played with just a collection of three or four chords, and in this chapter, we will look at the main ones.

There are seven notes in music, and chords are named after these. Chords are MAJOR* chords unless otherwise stated. Major chords make a kind of complete sound, whereas the other main form, MINOR* chords, make a sort of questioning, unfinished sound. Once you play one of each, the difference will be clear.

There are numerous varieties after that, but for this book, as it is for beginners, we will stick to just one alternative, a 7th chord*. This is a chord with an extra note (a seventh above the base note, for those interested).

The chords below are the ones that appear most commonly. Some, such as for example, the B Major chord (B) will appear in later chapters because they require a barre to play.

A Chords

Here, the lowest E string is not strummed*, the other five strings are. Use your first finger to cover the four strings on the second fret, then press the bottom string with your little finger

A

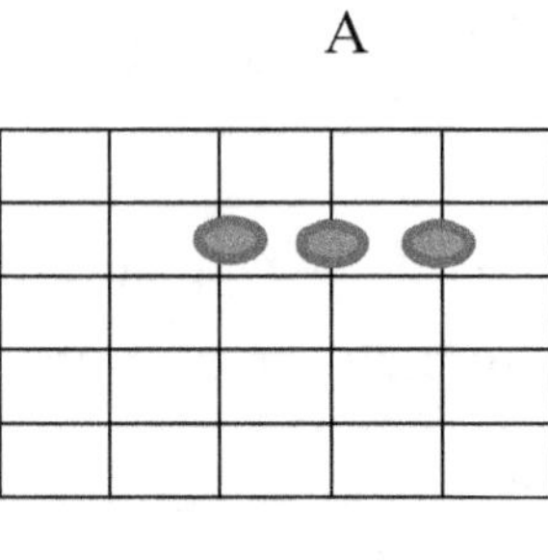

Am (A minor)

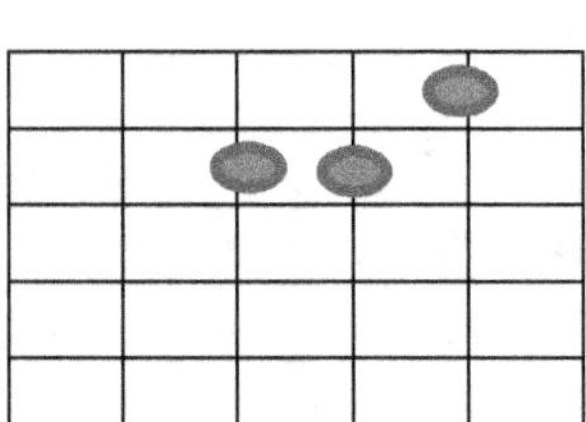

A7

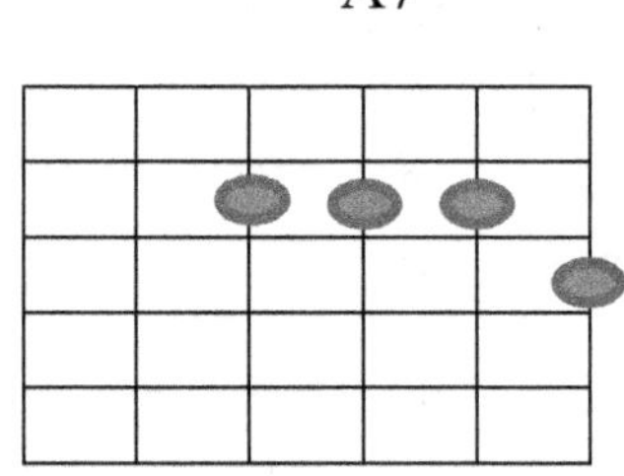

Use your first finger to cover the four strings on the second fret, then press the bottom string with your little finger

Am7

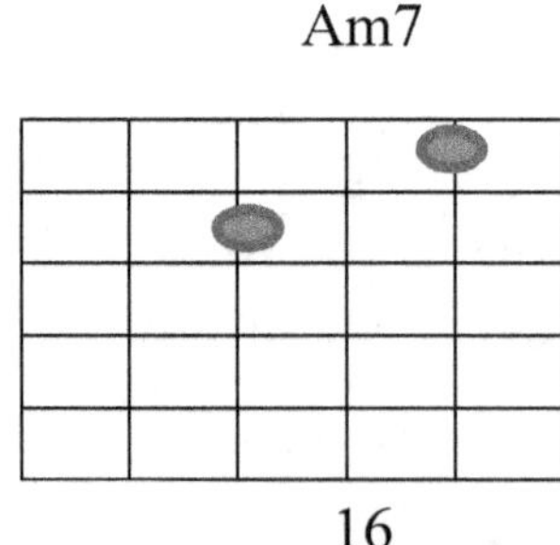

16

C Chords

As with A chords, the lowest E string is not strummed.

C

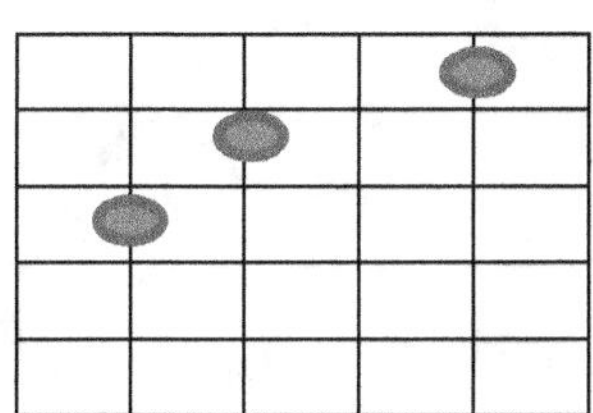

C7

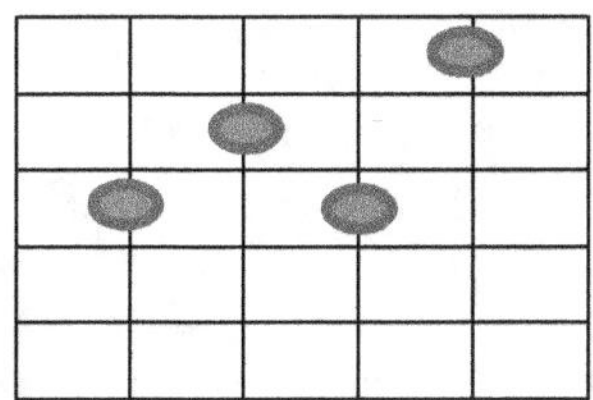

D Chords

Here, the lowest two strings, E and A, are not strummed.

D

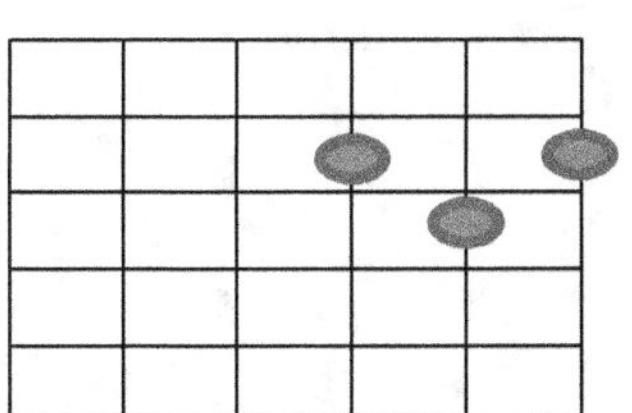

Dm

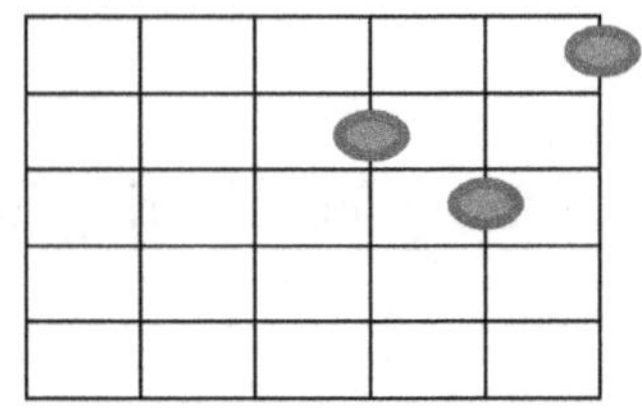

D7

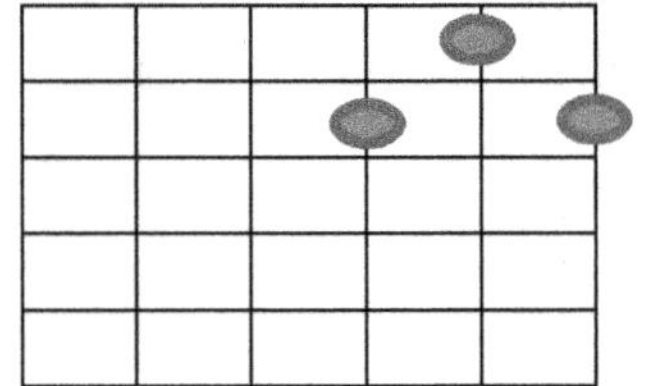

Dm7

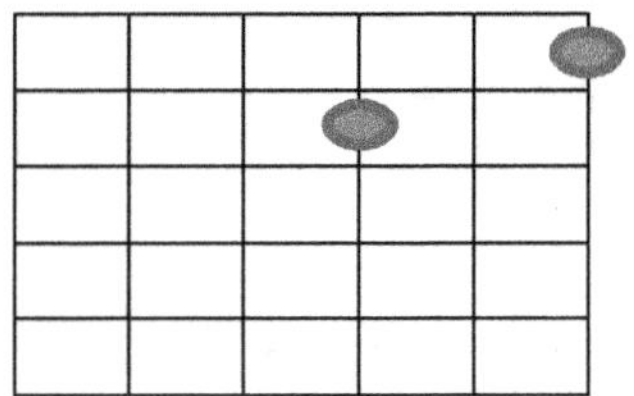

E Chords

Here, all strings are strummed.

E

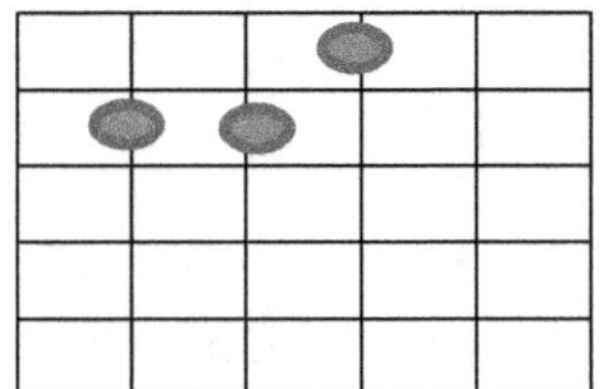

18

Em

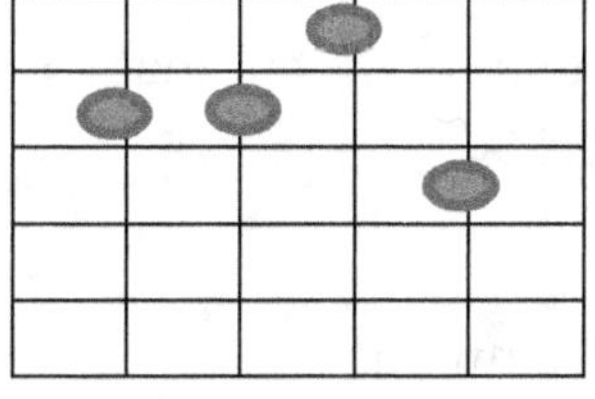

E7

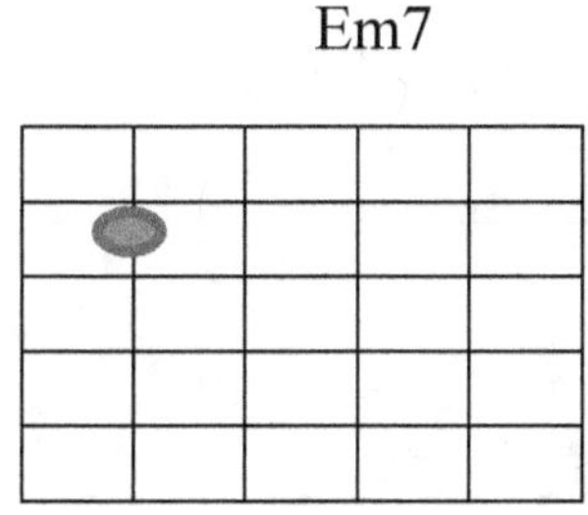

Use your first finger to cover the four strings on the second fret, then press the bottom string with your little finger

Em7

F Chords

If a barre is used, all strings are strummed, if not then the E and A strings are not strummed.

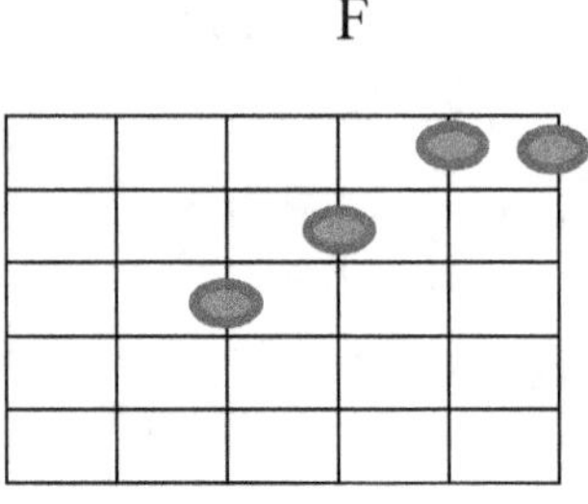

F

Use your first finger to hold down the first two strings. If you can, the first finger can create a bar by stretching over all six strings. It takes a bit of strength, but that soon develops.

G Chords

All strings are strummed.

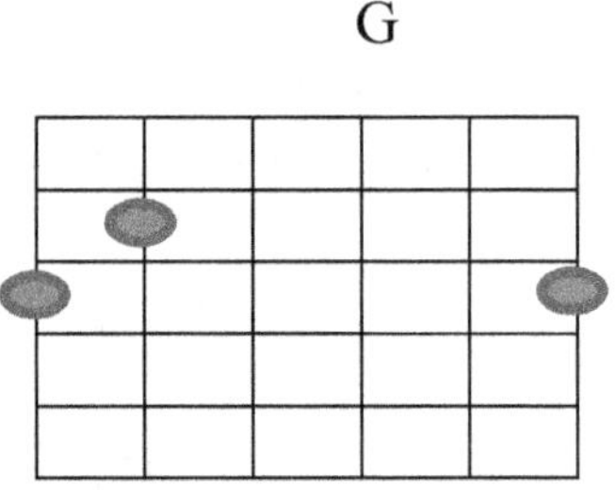

G

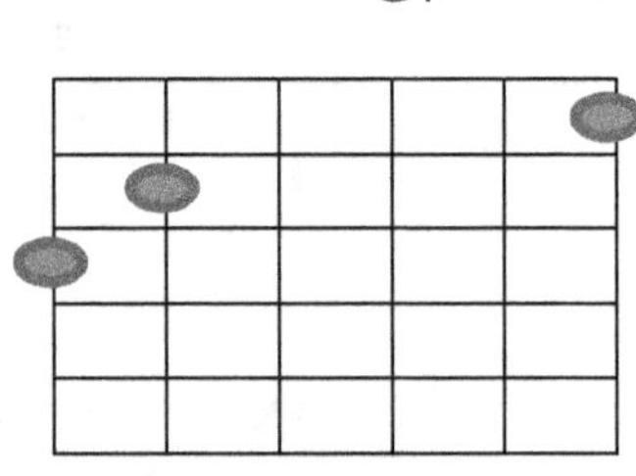

G7

The key with these chords is to practice them. Get them so that you can form each chord and play them so that there is no buzzing of the strings, or 'flat' sounds of a string not being pushed down firmly enough.

Progressions

Songs are often built around chord progressions. These are chords that simply go together well. Practice these and you will be able to use them in a wide range of songs.

The Most Common Progression

This works in any key, but for our purposes we will practice C, F and G

C C C C F F F F G G G G C C C C

Songs such as John Lennon's Imagine follow this progression.

Pop Progressions

These chord combinations work in popular songs such as Someone Like You by Adele. The chords are C, G, Am and F.

C C C C G G G G Am Am Am Am F F F F C C C C etc

Jazz Progressions

Everything from Boyfriend, the Justin Bieber, ummm, song and some of Queen's Bohemian Rhapsody follow this progression, which features the chords Dm, G and C.

Dm Dm Dm Dm G G G G C C C C Dm Dm Dm Dm etc

The Progression from the Fifties

Common in fact from the 1940s to the 1960s for both ballads and more upbeat songs, there are two progressions here. Firstly, is C Am Dm and G and songs such as the Beatles' The Fool on the Hill used this.

C C C C Am Am Am Am Dm Dm Dm Dm G G G G C C C C

Similar to this is the second progression which was used by the late great Leonard Cohen in the much-recorded Hallelujah. Here, the chords of C Am F and G are used.

C C C C Am Am Am Am F F F F G G G G

Chapter Summary

In this Chapter, we have presented all the most common chords that do not require a barre.

- These chords come in the major form, which is usually known just by its letter, that is, C is the same as C major
- They come in a seventh form
- The can also come in a minor form as well as a minor seventh version

- Chords are often put together in what are called progressions, and which form the basis of many songs.

In the next chapter you will learn a little bit about strumming.

Chapter Three: Lesson Three - Strumming

Before reading any further, give yourself a bit of a treat. Put your favourite CD, record, iPod song or whatever on to play. Listen carefully to the rhythm and count the beats of the drum. Sometimes, you can hear this on the guitars as well, but the drum is usually clearest.

What you are listening to is the beat of the song, sometimes called the time signature. In other words, the number of beats in a bar of music. If you learn to read music, this will be very important to help you play, but for the moment, just understanding about different rhythms in the simplest form is all that is needed.

Tap along to the beat, get that rhythm in your bones. What you will notice is that most, but not all, songs are written in 4/4 timing, that means that there are four beats in the bar. They might be played as eight quick beats, or two heavy and two light ones, or just 1,2,3,4; by counting or tapping your foot along you will see that the song is divided into blocks of four.

There are other rhythms, 3/4 is the beat of the waltz – **dum**, dee, dee, **dum**, dee, dee, **dum**, dee, dee, **dum**, dee, dee, etc. But we will start with four beats to the bar.

One tool here that can be very useful is a metronome, which is a device which ticks a steady rhythm out. You can buy a modern digital one from about $16, or a traditional one with a lever for about $100, which also makes a great ornament.

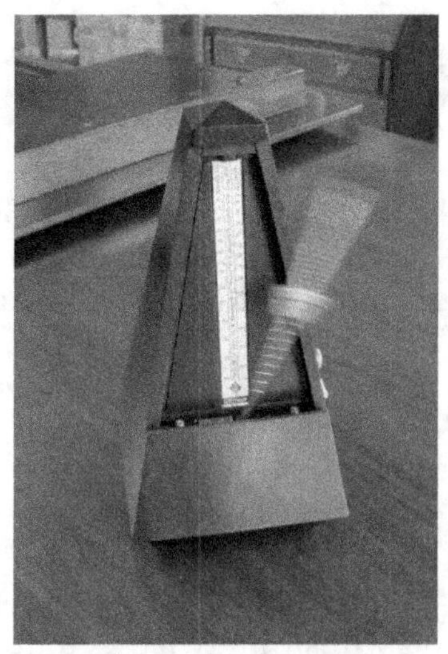

Or, there are apps available for your phone and free online versions. What the metronome will do, as it clicks away at the speed you set, is to help you keep a constant beat. This is really important as the guitar frequently supplies the rhythm for a song.

Basic Four-Four Rhythms

For each of the following, start by using you thumb, then add in a forefinger if it feels comfortable, finally, try it with a plectrum*.

Hold a chord that you feel comfortable making, and when you get the feel change the chord after ever bar, or four beats.

Set the metronome to sixty beats per minute, then when you get the hang of the rhythm, increase it to eighty beats per minute.

Example One

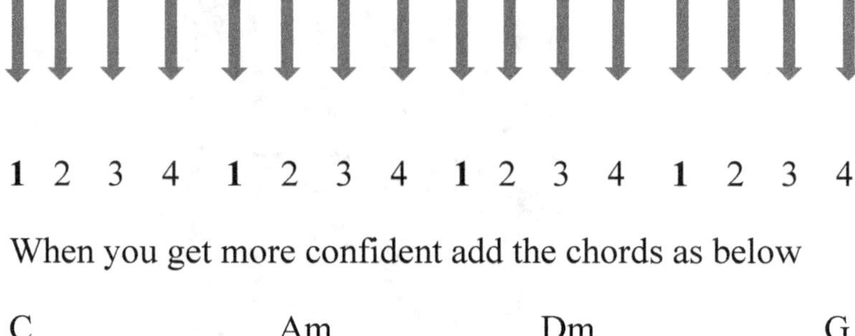

When you get more confident add the chords as below

C   Am   Dm   G

Example Two

This time you will strum twice as quickly, getting eight strokes in each four beats. Start with a down beat / strum and follow it with an upbeat. Once again, add the different chords when you have the hang of it. Don't forget to use your metronome to make sure you maintain a rhythm and keep time.

Example Three

Once you have these basics, then we can go for something very complicated. After you have mastered this and the chords we have shown you, you really will be able to call yourself a guitar player. Perhaps not yet an Eric Clapton, Jimi Hendrix or Paul Simon, but definitely someone who can bash out a beat, play the chords and make it sound good.

As before, start with the single chord and the slow speed, then build things up. Note the direction of the strokes.

Note that here the first 'stroke' of the third beat does not happen. The effect you are looking to achieve is **DUM   DEE DEE pause DEE DEE DEE DUM   DEE DEE pause DEE DEE DEE** etc.

A Tip for the Plectrum

It is best to start with a medium weight plectrum, as they are easiest to manipulate. Heavy ones can get caught on the strings, and lightweight ones can be harder to control. Hold the plectrum between your thumb and first finger, and curl the other fingers up into a loose fist. Hold the plectrum towards the top, so just over half is exposed to strike the strings. You do not want the strings to catch on your fingers.

Finally, remember when strumming that the movement comes from the wrist, not the whole arm. The great arm flashing helicopter rotors of Pete Townshend and other performers are for show, not effect. Just a small rotation of the wrist leads to controlled, pure strumming with a great sound.

Chapter Summary

In this chapter we have learned a little about strumming, the technique and some rhythms that can be played.

In the next chapter we will learn something a little more technical: reading tabs.

Chapter Four: Lesson Four - Reading Tabs

There are four basic ways to play the notes and chords, found in a piece of music, on the guitar. These are:

- Reading the Music
- Playing by Ear
- Reading Chord Names
- Playing by Tab

Reading Music

The guitar is unusual when it comes to instruments. First, compared to most, it is relatively easy to learn. There is none of the complex finger movements of the piano, breathing challenges of wind and brass instruments or judgement of tone and pitch associated with the likes of the violin and cello.

That means that players are often self-taught, from books such as this, or have picked it up from friends. Learning to read music is a very useful skill indeed, but it is time consuming and needs a lot of practice. It tends to be an element left out when learning the guitar without the benefit of formal tutorage.

However, there is a use in knowing where the various notes are located on the guitar. These are presented in the table below. Along the top are the fret positions, down the side are the strings to which the fret position is related and finally in the middle is the note played. The logical pattern will quickly become apparent. Remember that the following pairs of notes are the same:

A# and Bb, C# and Db, D# and Eb, F# and Gb, G# and Ab

Open	First	Second	Third	Fourth	Fifth	Sixth	Seventh	Eighth
E (first)	F	F#	G	G#	A	Bb	B	C
B (second)	C	C#	D	Eb	E	F	F#	G
G (third)	G#	A	Bb	B	C	C#	D	Eb
D (fourth)	Eb	E	F	F#	G	G#	A	Bb
A (fifth)	Bb	B	C	C#	D	Eb	E	F
E (sixth)	F	F#	G	G#	A	Bb	B	C

Playing by Ear

There are some natural musicians who can just hear a piece, and know how to play it and which chords or notes to use. Sadly, not many of us fit into that category.

Playing by Chords

This is the easiest way of playing. Here, the chords to play are written above the lyrics of the song. The only problem is that if you do not know the song, it can be very hard to play. Getting the placement of the actual chord changes is also very difficult. Simply placing the fingers in the exact place is a challenge. There are some songs using this method later in the book, to get players started.

Playing by Tab

This might seem complicated at first, but with a bit of time, can be a very helpful way of overcoming the difficulties listed above.

The tab is a horizontal box with six lines, each one equating to one of the guitar's strings. The lowest represents the low E string, next is the A string, the D string, G string, then one from the top is the B string, with the top line equating to the higher pitched E string.

Numbers printed on the strings relate to the fret that the string should be played on. A '0' means that the string should be played open.

Chords are a little more complicated, but still quick to learn. Here, numbers appear on all the strings.

Can you work out which chord the following tablature represents?

It is, of course, E major. Strings 1 (E), 2 (B) and 6 (E) are open, then the G string is played on the first fret, and strings 4 and 5, (D and A) are played on the second fret.

To help even more, tablature, or tabs, will usually feature the chord's name as well.

A little later we will learn a bit about finger picking. This is when the notes of the chord are played individually by the fingers of, for right handed players, the right hand. The proper name for this is an arpeggiated chord*.

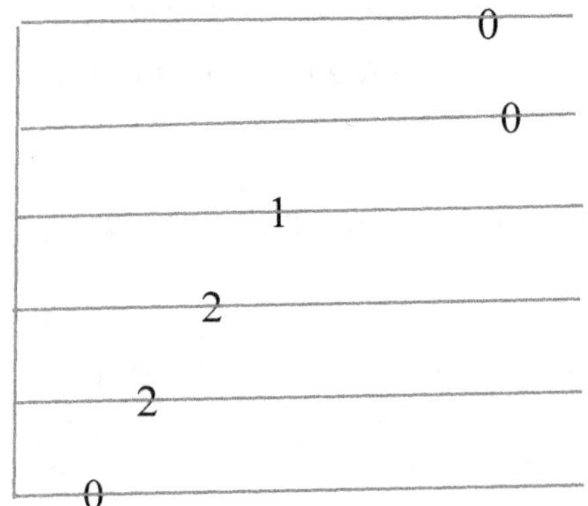

The arpeggiated E major chord will look like the diagram above.

Where a string should not be played, it is indicated by an X. There are numerous other signs in tablature, which can be investigated when a player is more competent with their instrument, but this is enough information for the first stages of playing, especially as this book aims to get players up and running, at the most basic level, within a day.

Chapter Summary

In this chapter we have learned four ways of playing the guitar. By chord, by ear, by music and by tab.

- Playing by chord is the most straightforward, but is a rough science.
- Tab and music are accurate, but trickier (especially by music).
- Playing by ear is an aptitude all musicians would like, but few possess.

In the next chapter we talk about barre chords, the method by which any chord can be played.

Chapter Five: Lesson Five - Barre Chords

In this chapter you will learn about how the barre can turn the basic chord shapes into any chord.

Creating the barre can be tiring at first, and strength needs to build up in the hand. It is easiest on an electric guitar, where the neck is slim and the strings are usually lightweight. The Spanish guitar is hardest because of the width of the neck and the bulkiness of the strings.

Below we can see how the basic E chord fingering turns into the chord of F when it is shifted down a fret, and the index finger makes a barre behind it.

F

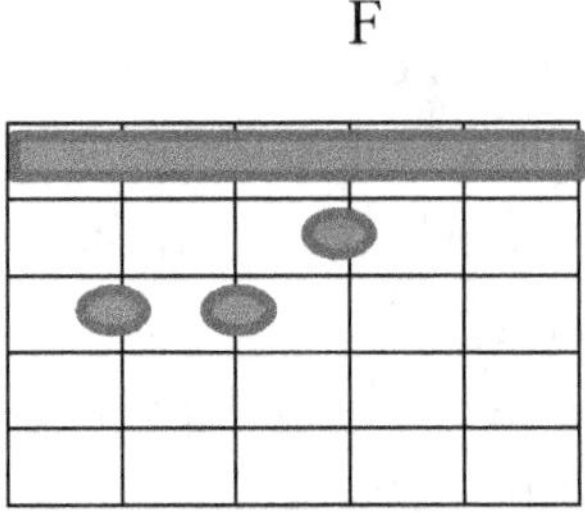

Here are some of the chords that we did not show earlier, with their barre in place

B Chords

B

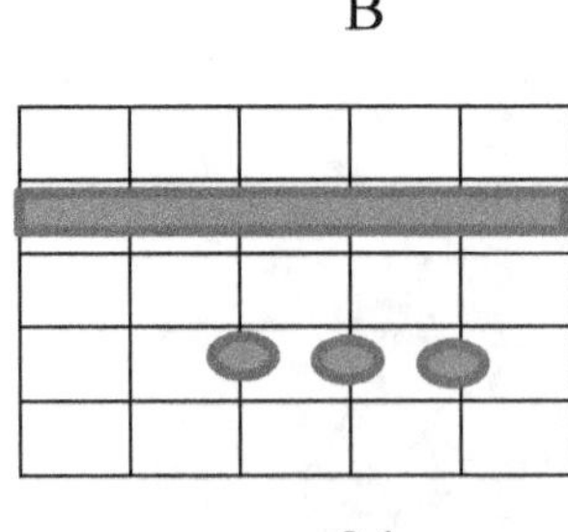

Bm

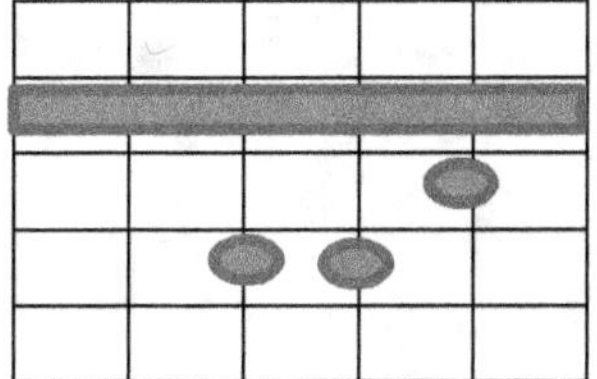

B7 (no low E strummed)

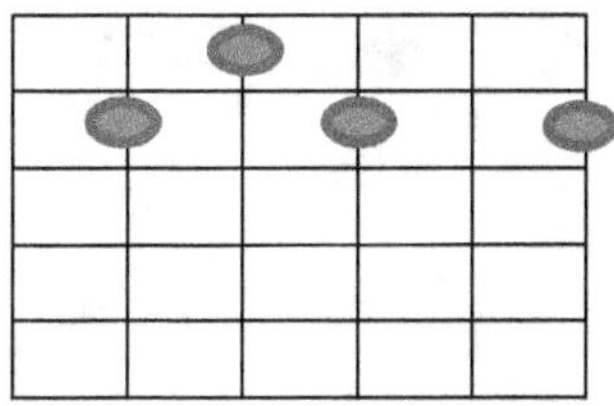

Bm7

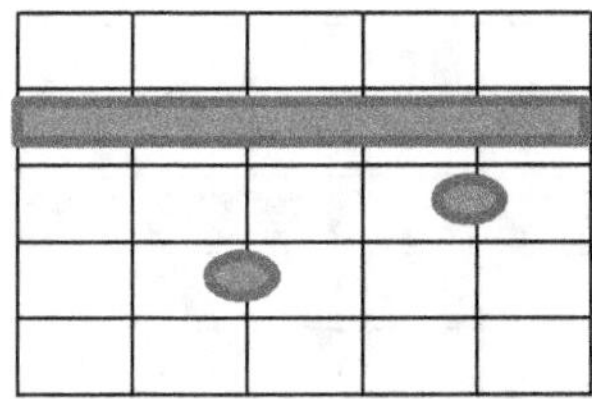

F Chords

Fm

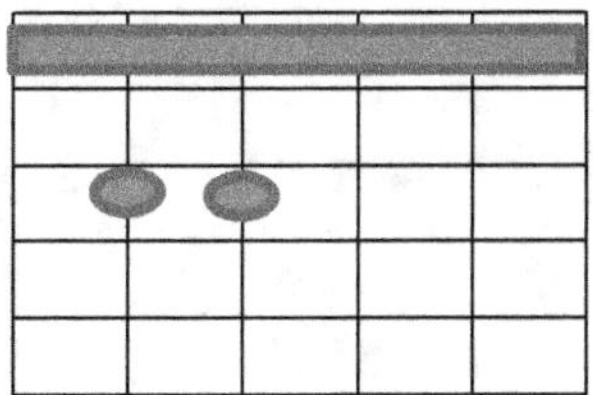

F7

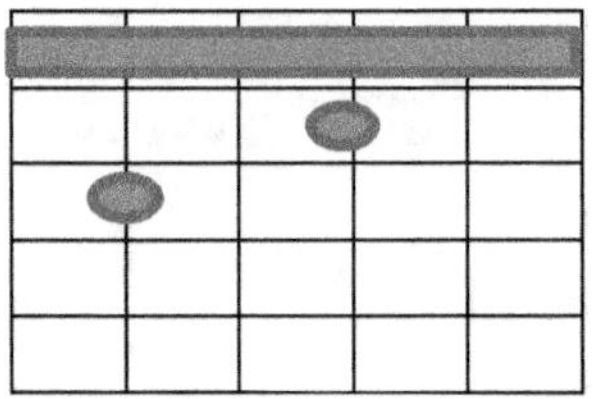

Fm7

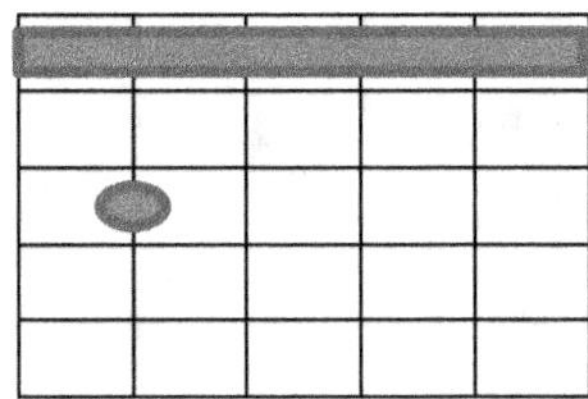

G Chords

Gm

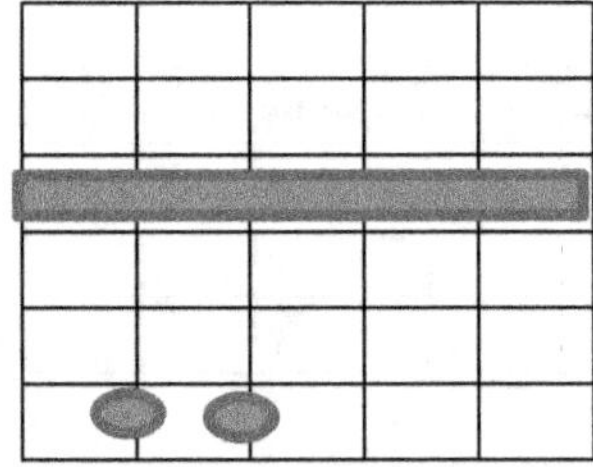

Gm7

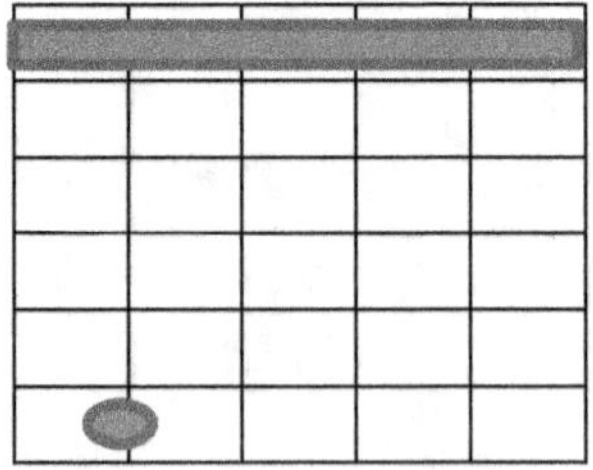

Sharps and Flats

Sharp and flat chords tend to be made using a barre. The most common chords here are F sharp (F#), C#, B flat (Bb) and Eb, although there are several more.

F#

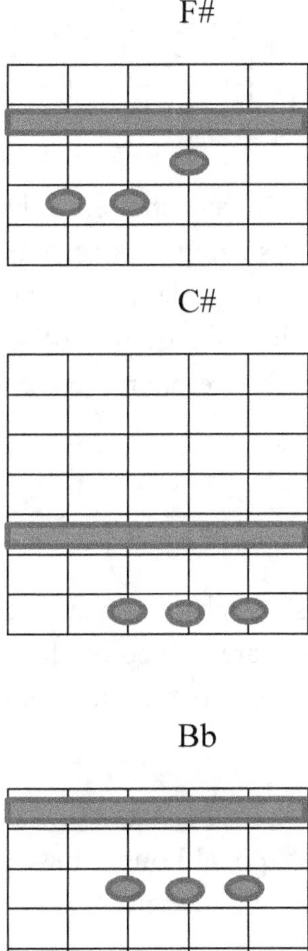

C#

Bb

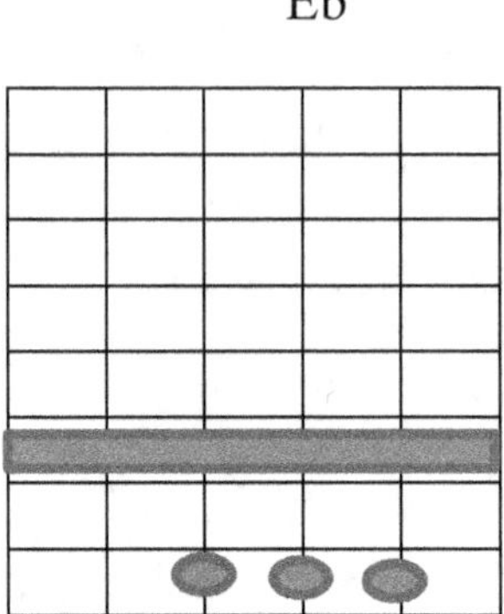

As many of you will have spotted, it is possible to play the same chord in many ways using a barre. This can make chord changes easier as players become more experienced. Although the chord is the same, the pitch and quality of sound will vary depending on where on the fretboard* the chord is played.

Chord Table

The table below shows how various chords are formed depending on where they are played on the fretboard. Chord shapes are listed across the top, and the fret on which the barre is held down the side.

In the middle is the chord that is formed. The pattern can be repeated for any cord shape, although these are the shapes that are usually to be found used with a barre.

	E	Em	Em7	A	Am	Am7
1st	F	Fm	Fm7	Bb	Bbm	Bbm7
2nd	F#	F#m	F#m7	B	Bm	Bm7
3rd	G	Gm	Gm7	C	Cm	Cm7
4th	Ab	G#m	G#m7	C#	C#m	C#m7
5th	A	Am	Am7	D	Dm	Dm7
6th	Bb	Bbm	Bbm7	Eb	Ebm	Ebm7
7th	B	Bm	Bm7	E	Em	Em7
8th	C	Cm	Cm7	F	Fm	Fm7

Chapter Summary

In this chapter we have looked at the barre.

- We have seen that the barre accompanied by the shapes of other chords can create new chords.

- Practising with a barre makes chord changes easier.

In the next chapter you will learn more about those essentials of instrument playing, scales.

Chapter Six: Lesson Six - Guitar Scales

Quite a short chapter this one, but a very important one. Scales are the notes that are contained within a particular key in music. Songs are written in keys, and by knowing the notes that are involved in that key, it is possible to play accompaniments and lead guitar to go with it.

A great way to warm up is to run through a couple of scales, it gets the fingers of both hands working, and over time the notes will become engrained in your head. You will then know, even if you are just reading the chords involved in a piece, the key in which it is based.

The tables below show the notes involved in all the major and minor keys. The numbers on the left indicate the place of that note in the scale, while the keys are across the top.

Major Keys

	A	Bb	B	C	Db	D	Eb	E	F	F#	G	Ab
1	A	Bb	B	C	Db	D	Eb	E	F	F#	G	Ab
2	B	C	Db	D	Eb	E	F	F#	G	G#	A	Bb
3	C#	D	Eb	E	F	F#	G	G#	A	Bb	B	C
4	D	Eb	E	F	F#	G	Ab	A	Bb	B	C	Db
5	E	F	F#	G	Ab	A	Bb	B	C	C#	D	Eb
6	F#	G	Ab	A	Bb	B	C	C#	D	D#	E	F
7	Ab	A	Bb	B	C	C#	D	D#	E	F	F#	G
8	A	Bb	B	C	Db	D	Eb	E	F	F#	G	Ab

Minor Keys (Harmonic Minors)

	A m	Bb m	B m	C m	C# m	D m	Eb m	E m	F m	F# m	G m	G# m
1	A	Bb	B	C	C#	D	Eb	E	F	F#	G	G#
2	B	C	C	D	D#	E	F	F#	G	G#	A	A
3	C	Db	D	Eb	E	F	Gb	G	Ab	A	Bb	B
4	D	Eb	E	f	F#	G	Ab	A	Bb	B	C	C#
5	E	F	F#	G	G#	A	Bb	B	C	C#	D	D#
6	F	Gb	G	Ab	A	Bb	C	C	Db	D	E	E
7	G#	A	Bb	B	C	C#	D	D#	E	F	F#	G
8	A	Bb	B	C	C#	D	Eb	E	F	F#	G	G#

There are many different types of minor scales, such as harmonic (which is printed), melodic and natural scales. However, the harmonic is fine for using at the level we are currently at.

One of the most common and popular scales for the guitar is the blues scale.

The blues scale in C includes the following notes:

C	Eb	F	Gb	G	**Bb**	C

In the key of D, it looks like this:

D	F	G	Ab	A	C	D

Finally, we will learn the classic series of notes that, once mastered, lead to the classic 12 bar blues themes that underpin so many songs.

In tab form, it looks like this:

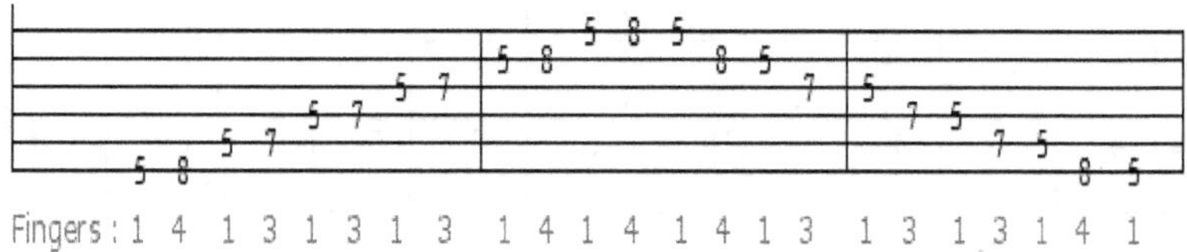

In notes, it is played as follows:

↑	A	C	D	E	G	A	C	D	E	G	A	C	↓
A	G	E	D	C	A	G	E	D	C	A			

Chapter Summary

Chapter six has introduced you to the concept of the musical scale. You have been given the notes involved in the different key signatures in which music is written.

In the next chapter you will learn more about plectrums or picks, and a little about finger picking.

Chapter Seven: Lesson Seven - Using a Plectrum and Finger Picking

As we saw earlier, there are many different weights of plectrum. It is best to start strumming with a middle weight one, and over time players will find the weight that suits them best, and which works for the kind of music they are playing. Heavy plectrums tend to be easier for picking notes if, for example, a combination of picking and strumming is required. Lightweight plectrums are handy for faster, smoother strumming. They are handy for electric guitars, where the sound is created electronically.

There are also thumb and finger picks which can be worn when picking notes. They can be tricky to use, catching on the strings, and a light action is needed. As a beginner, it is probably best to start picking using the fingers, rather than the picks shown below, but it is a matter of choice. A sharper sound is created with the picks.

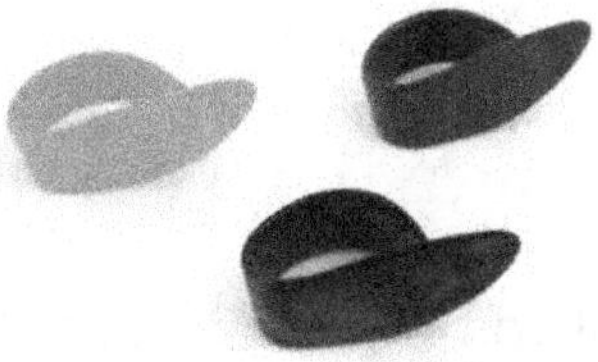

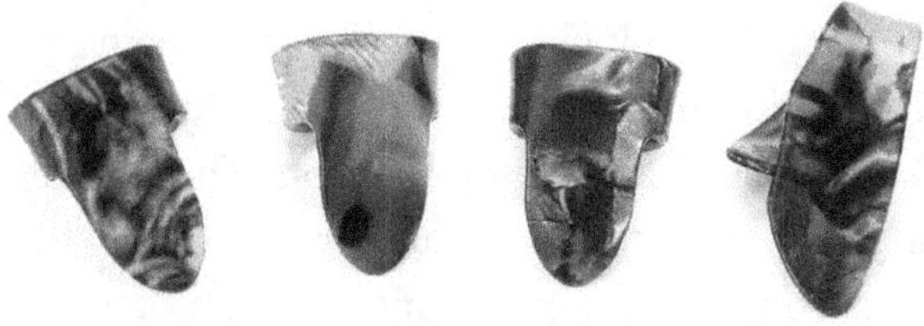

Whether picking or strumming, a different tone is created depending on where the action takes place. Playing over the sound hole (or pick up, with an electric guitar) creates the fullest, and loudest sound.

Move towards the bridge, and a harsher tone is produced. Unsurprisingly, playing closer to the neck makes for a softer, more mellifluous sound.

Finger Picking

Sometimes called finger style*, or plucking*, this is the method by which individual notes of a chord are played one after the other, often quite quickly. It is a style often associated with folk style music, and ballads.

Listen to Paul Simon playing the opening to the Simon and Garfunkel hit, The Boxer, to hear finger picking at its best.

Picking usually works as follows. The thumb plays any notes on the low E, A and D strings, while the first, second and third fingers pick notes from the G, B and E strings. Normally, the index finger will pluck the lowest string being played, usually the G string, with the middle finger next, usually the B string and the third finger used for the top E string. The little finger is not used, and many players place it under the sound hole on the body of the guitar to provide support and help the other fingers to remain in the correct place. The only time it would come into play is if there is a need to pluck five strings simultaneously.

Picking can be used with arpeggiated chords, and for playing pairs of notes together

An advantage of finger picking is that it turns the guitar into more than a percussive rhythm keeper. It allows for melodies to be interspersed with chords, and for the playing of harmonies (notes combined to produce a pleasing effect). Hammers* and pull offs* can also be incorporated into playing, as the guitarist becomes more competent. Tapping the body of the guitar to create a percussion effect is also easier than when working with a plectrum.

It is still possible to strum, using the thumb or first finger, but the sound created has a different quality to that created with a pick, and therefore it is not suitable for more upbeat rockier numbers.

Finger pickers need to keep their hands in good condition. The right hand always needs short finger nails for pressing the strings, and the same is true for the finger picker, unless they choose to use artificial picks. A nail too long will catch on the string, spoiling the effect being sought.

Another advantage with finger picking is that a greater variety of sound can be created. Generally, the volume will be lower, but varying the position of where the strings are plucked, and the force with which this happens, can alter the timbre*, to create mood and atmosphere in a song.

More flexibility is offered when playing, flamenco style strumming, plucking of multiple strings, arpeggios and such like all are easier to play with fingerpicking. However, the strings used should be nylon or light gauge steel, unless an artificial pick is attached to the fingers, to prevent nail and finger damage.

All the above makes it clear that finger picking lends itself to classical, solo guitar playing or playing as an accompaniment to voice or just perhaps one or two other instruments.

When finger picking is notarised in a piece of music, it will usually adopt the following notations:

Thumb = B

Index = I

Middle = M

Ring = A

Little = C or X or E

What's Next

As with everything else when learning the guitar, practice is all.

There are two simple finger picking exercises that can be practised to get the player into the swing.

For each, use the thumb for the E, A and D strings, the index finger for the G string, middle finger for the B string and third finger for the top E.

Use the chord progressions from earlier to practice. Set the metronome for 60 – it can get faster as you progress.

The first pattern is for 3/4 timing, the second for 4/4.

We will use the Dm, C, G, Dm progression in the example below. We will be playing two strings for each beat of the bar.

It goes something like this:

3/4 Example

The top row represents the chord, the second the finger playing and the third is the beat.

Dm						C						G						Dm					
T	I	M	A	M	I	T	I	M	A	M	I	T	I	M	A	M	I	T	I	M	A	M	I
1		2		3		1		2		3		1		2		3		1		2		3	

And so on…

4/4 Example

Dm								C								G							
T	I	M	A	M	I	T	I	T	I	M	A	M	I	T	I	T	I	M	A	M	I	T	I
1		2		3		4		1		2		3		4		1		2		3		4	

Chapter Summary

In this chapter we have learned a bit about finger picking, its uses and tools that can help.

- We know about how the notation is present
- We have undertaken some practice
- We know the kind of music with which it works best.

In the next chapter we will present some songs for you to play.

Chapter Eight: Some Songs to Play

Below are some songs along with their chords. They are well known, and if one is unfamiliar, they can be found easily on the internet. For legal reasons, we can only print songs that are out of copywrite, but there are hundreds of examples of popular music on the internet, plus countless books available from your local music stores.

Sing along with the songs, it will help you to 'feel' where the changes take place and keep you in time.

Happy Birthday

    A   E
Happy Birthday to you
    D   A
Happy Birthday to you
    A7   D
Happy Birthday dear Billy (please feel free to substitute a
name!)
    A   E   A
Happy Birthday to you.

Morning Has Broken

```
        C  Dm  G          F   C
Morning has broken, like the first morning
(C)         Em  Am  D7      D   G
Blackbird has spoken, like the first bird
C         F     C          Am   D
Praise for the singing, praise for the morning
G           C  F  G7         C     F
Praise for the springing fresh from the world
[Interlude]
G E  Am  G  C  G7
            C  Dm   G        F   C
Sweet the rain's new fall, sunlit from heaven
(C)         Em  Am  D7      D   G
Like the first dewfall, on the first grass
C          F   C          Am   D
Praise for the sweetness of the wet garden
G           C  F  G7         C     F
Sprung in completeness where his feet pass
[Interlude]
G  E  Am  F#  Bm  G  D  A7/D  D
         D  Em   A        G   D
Mine is the sunlight, mine is the morning
         F#m Bm     E7        A
Born of the one light, Eden saw play
D         G    D        Bm  E
Praise with elation, praise every morning
A        D G  A7      D
God's recreation of the new day
```

G A F# Bm G7 C F C

        C Dm G   F   C
Morning has broken, like the first morning
(C)   Em Am D7   D   G
Blackbird has spoken, like the first bird
C   F   C   Am D
Praise for the singing, praise for the morning
G   C F G7   C   F
Praise for the springing fresh from the world
[Outro]
G E Am F# Bm G D A7/D D

She'll Be Coming Round the Mountain

G
She'll be coming 'round the mountain
     G
When she comes.
      G
She'll be coming 'round the mountain
     D7
When she comes.
     G
She'll be coming 'round the mountain,
     C
She'll be coming 'round the mountain,
    G   D7
She'll be coming 'round the mountain,
     G
When she comes.

[Verse 2]
     G
She'll be driving six white horses
     G
When she comes
     G
She'll be driving six white horses
    D7
When she comes
       G
She'll be driving six white horses
       C

She'll be driving six white horses
              G   D7
She'll be driving six white horses
        G
When she comes

[Verse 3]
        G
Oh, we'll all come out to meet her
        G
When she comes
        G
Oh, we'll all come out to meet her
        D7
When she comes
        G
Oh, we'll all come out to meet her
        C
Oh, we'll all come out to meet her
        G   D7
Oh, we'll all come out to meet her
        G
When she comes

[Verse 4]
        G
We will kill the old red rooster
        G
When she comes
        G
We will kill the old red rooster
        D7

When she comes
      G
We will kill the old red rooster
      C
We will kill the old red rooster
      G   D7
We will kill the old red rooster
      G
When she comes

[Verse 5]
      G
We'll all have chicken n' dumplin's
        G
When she comes
      G
We'll all have chicken n' dumplin's
        D7
When she comes
        G
We'll all have chicken n' dumplin's
        C
We'll all have chicken n' dumplin's
      G   D7
We'll all have chicken n' dumplin's
        G
When she comes

Swing Low, Sweet Chariot

<pre>
C
I looked over Jordan,
   F   C
And what did I see,
                    G7
Comin' for to carry me home,
  C   F   C
A band of angels comin' after me,
          G7   C
Comin' for to carry me home.

        C   F   C
Swing Low, sweet chariot,
                    G7
Comin' for to carry me home;
          C   F   C
Swing low, sweet chariot,
C   G7   C
Comin' for to carry me home.
</pre>

The Drunken Sailor

Em
What shall we do with the drunken sailor?
D
What shall we do with the drunken sailor?
Em
What shall we do with the drunken sailor?

[Chorus]

Em D   Em
Ear-ly in the morning
Em
Hooray, and up she rises
D
Hooray, and up she rises
Em
Hooray, and up she rises
Em D   Em
Ear-ly in the morning

[Verse]

Em
Put him in the long boat 'til he's sober
D
Put him in the long boat 'til he's sober
Em
Put him in the long boat 'til he's sober

[Chorus]

Em D   Em
Ear-ly in the morning
Em
Hooray, and up she rises
D
Hooray, and up she rises
Em
Hooray, and up she rises
Em D   Em
Ear-ly in the morning

[Verse]

Em
Pull out the plug and wet him all over
D
Pull out the plug and wet him all over
Em
Pull out the plug and wet him all over

[Chorus]

Em D   Em
Ear-ly in the morning
Em
Hooray, and up she rises
D
Hooray, and up she rises

Hooray, and up she rises

Em
Hooray, and up she rises
Em D   Em
Ear-ly in the morning

[Verse]

Em
Put him in the bilge and make him drink it
D
Put him in the bilge and make him drink it
Em
Put him in the bilge and make him drink it

[Chorus]

Em D   Em
Ear-ly in the morning
Em
Hooray, and up she rises
D
Hooray, and up she rises
Em
Hooray, and up she rises
Em D   Em
Ear-ly in the morning

[Verse]

Em
Put him in a leaky boat and make him bale her
D
Put him in a leaky boat and make him bale her
Em
Put him in a leaky boat and make him bale her

[Chorus]

Em D   Em
Ear-ly in the morning
Em
Hooray, and up she rises
D
Hooray, and up she rises
Em
Hooray, and up she rises
Em D   Em
Ear-ly in the morning

[Verse]

Em
Tie him to the scuppers with the hose pipe on him
D
Tie him to the scuppers with the hose pipe on him
Em
Tie him to the scuppers with the hose pipe on him

[Chorus]

Em D   Em
Ear-ly in the morning
Em
Hooray, and up she rises
D
Hooray, and up she rises
Em
Hooray, and up she rises
Em D   Em
Ear-ly in the morning

[Verse]

Em
Shave his belly with a rusty razor
D
Shave his belly with a rusty razor
Em
Shave his belly with a rusty razor

[Chorus]

Em D   Em
Ear-ly in the morning
Em
Hooray, and up she rises
D
Hooray, and up she rises

Em
Hooray, and up she rises
Em D   Em
Ear-ly in the morning

[Verse]

Em
Tie him to the topmast while she's yardarm under
D
Tie him to the topmast while she's yardarm under
Em
Tie him to the topmast while she's yardarm under

[Chorus]

Em D   Em
Ear-ly in the morning
Em
Hooray, and up she rises
D
Hooray, and up she rises
Em
Hooray, and up she rises
Em D   Em
Ear-ly in the morning

[Verse]

Em
Heave him by the leg in a runnin' bowline
D
Heave him by the leg in a runnin' bowline
Em
Heave him by the leg in a runnin' bowline

[Chorus]

Em D   Em
Ear-ly in the morning
Em
Hooray, and up she rises
D
Hooray, and up she rises
Em
Hooray, and up she rises
Em D   Em
Ear-ly in the morning

[Verse]

Em
Keel haul him 'til he's sober
D
Keel haul him 'til he's sober
Em
Keel haul him 'til he's sober

[Chorus]

Em D   Em
Ear-ly in the morning
Em
Hooray, and up she rises
D
Hooray, and up she rises
Em
Hooray, and up she rises
Em D   Em
Ear-ly in the morning

Greensleeves

Am   C
Alas my love,
  G   Em
you do me wrong,
  Am   E
to cast me off so discourteously,
  Am   C   G   Em
for I have loved you so long,
  Am   E7   Am
delighting in your company.

[Chorus]

C   G   Em
greensleeves was all my joy,
Am   E
greensleeves was my delight,
C   G   Em
greensleeves was my heart of gold,
  Am   E7 Am
and who but my lady greensleeves.

[Verse 2]

  Am   C   G   Em
Thy gown was of the grassy green,
  Am   E
Thy sleeves of satin hanging by,

    Am   C   G   Em
Which made thee be our harvest queen,
 Am   E7   Am
And yet thou wouldst not love me.

[Chorus]

C   G   Em
greensleeves was all my joy,
Am   E
greensleeves was my delight,
C   G   Em
greensleeves was my heart of gold,
   Am   E7 Am
and who but my lady greensleeves.

[Verse 3]

 Am   C   G   Em
Well, I will pray to God on high,
    Am   E
That thou constancy mayst see,
 Am   C   G   Em
And that yet once before I die,
Am   E7   Am
Thou will vouchsafe to love me.

Jingle Bells

```
C
Dashing through the snow
                F
In a one horse open sleigh
              G
O'er the fields we go
                C
Laughing all the way
C
Bells on bob tails ring
                F
Making spirits bright
F           G
What fun it is to laugh and sing
G           C
A sleighing song tonight


C
Oh, jingle bells, jingle bells
C
Jingle all the way
F           C
Oh, what fun it is to ride
G
In a one horse open sleigh
C
Jingle bells, jingle bells
C
Jingle all the way
F                 C
```

Oh, what fun it is to ride
G   (F)   C
In a one horse open sleigh

Chapter Nine: Stringing and Tuning Your Guitar

Playing the guitar when it has new strings is always a treat. The beautiful sounds of the strings and the quality of the notes make it seem as though you are playing a new instrument. However, fitting the little blighters is not such fun.

Remember, classical or Spanish guitars have nylon or gut strings, other varieties take steel strings. Put steel strings on a Spanish guitar and the stresses will be too much, resulting in damage to the body and neck.

If you are not going to be playing the guitar for a while, loosen the tension on the strings, it helps to take the pressure off the guitar's frame.

Restringing a Guitar

Little intricacies around the bridge can vary from guitar to guitar, but the basics are below.

Step One

Turn the tuning peg, loosening each of the existing strings, until all are quiet slack.

Step Two

Starting with the Low E string, keep loosening until the string can be pushed through its hole. Then, pull it out from the bridge. This may involve untying a knot, pulling by the little nut on the end of the string, or removing a string holder from the bridge by pulling, it will depend on your guitar.

Step Three

Repeat step two with all the other strings, starting with the A string, then through D, G, B and finishing with E.

Step Four

Take the bottom E string, the lowest note (it will be the thickest string, in its own little pack). Push the end through the hole in the bridge, and pull tight. Secure the string with whatever means the old string was secured by. Slide the string through the hole in its tuning peg, making sure that you have it in the correct peg. This first string will go through the first hole in the head at the top of the guitar.

Step Five

Pull the string tight, then feedback about 4-6 cm to create some slack.

Step Six

At the head end, angle the string slightly upwards and turn the tuning peg to tighten it. When the string is taught enough, position it in its slot in the nut of the guitar. That is the small, slotted strip where the neck meets the head. Tighten further until the string is sufficiently tense to remain in place in the nut. Don't worry about tuning yet.

Step Seven

Repeat steps four, five and six with the other strings, starting with the A string, then the D, G, B and finally the top E.

Step Eight

If you have excessive amounts of string hanging loose at the neck end, get some cutters and trim the strings. Leave about 3-4 cm showing.

You now have a restringed guitar…one that is very out of tune.

Tuning the Guitar

Unless you have purchased expensive, pre-stressed strings, then your guitar will go out of tune very quickly. You will need to retune regularly for a week or so. You will find that the guitar stays in tune for longer and longer periods.

First Tune

Unless you are blessed with perfect pitch, you will need something to tune the guitar to. A piano, tuning fork or measuring device attached to the head will do help you with this. Just as easy is to go online and search for a free guitar tuner. These work perfectly well.

Tuning the Guitar to itself

Once the instrument has settled after its re-stringing. It is much quicker to tune it to itself. This can be done in two ways.

Note Method

The fifth fret on the string is the same note as the open string on the next. So, pressing and playing the fifth fret on the A string, gives the note D, which is the same as the open D string.

The only exception is from the G string to the B string. Here, the fourth fret needs to be played to get the same note, B, as the open string after it.

Tune the string while holding down the note and letting both it and the open note ring on. Although requiring a bit of contortion, this allows you to hear the notes blend together.

Harmonic* Method

Harmonics are played by placing the finger of the left hand lightly on the string directly over a fret marker. The string is plucked and the finger lifted simultaneously. A bell like ringing sound is created.

Listening to the harmonics is a great way to tune, as rather than judging pitch, you will hear the vibrations of the harmonics. They will synch together when the notes are the same.

You will need to play harmonics on the fifth fret of the lower string, and seventh fret of the higher string to get the effect required. Unfortunately, this method does not work with the G to B strings, although it does with all other combinations.

Hearing Method

If you play a chord slowly, or two notes an octave* apart (use the table of notes in the earlier chapter to find where the same notes can be found) those with a good ear can hear whether their guitar is in tune or not. This gets easier with experience.

Tuning a Twelve String Guitar

If re-stringing a normal guitar is tricky, that is nothing to a 12 string. Tuning, too, is a little different.

For normal pitch, the main six strings are tuned as normal, but between each of the low E, A, D and G a string is fitted and pitched to an octave above the main note. The top two strings, B and top E, have their partners as identical pitch to themselves.

So, starting from the lowest string, the tuning is:

E (as per normal guitar)

E (up an octave)

A

A (up an octave)

D

D (up an octave)

G

G (up an octave)

B

B (same note, NOT up an octave)

E

E (same note, NOT up an octave)

Hard work, but a great sound.

Chapter Ten: Other Information

Types of Guitars

The main types are:

- *Spanish guitar*, usually the smallest kind, with nylon or gut strings, and a soft but precise sound. Usually finger picked, but can be strummed, usually with the thumb or fingers.
- *Acoustic Guitar*, steel stringed and usually finger picked or strummed with a plectrum.
- *Electric Acoustic*, as above with the addition of an electronic pick up to allow it to be played through an amplifier.
- *Electric Guitar*, often with one or two pick-ups, usually strummed or played as lead guitar – see below.
- *Bass Guitar*, four stringed electric with different tuning. Notes are usually plucked.
- *Combo*, a guitar with two necks allowing bass and normal guitar to be played.
- *Hollow Bodies Guitars* – these are electric guitars where the sound is enhanced with a hollow body. See below for an example.

- *Twelve String,* a steel strung acoustic usually strummed.
- *Hawaiian*, a guitar really in name only, although the steel tube with which the notes are formed can be bought for other guitar types.
- *Four and A Half String*, yes, really! Some of the earliest instruments were four stringed, with an extra, open string attached from the bridge to half way along the neck.

Looking After Your Guitar

You can get a decent, second hand model for $10, or you can pay thousands. Whichever, a guitar is a precision instrument and deserves to be treated as such. It is worth investing in a case to protect from everyday life. A soft one is fine if the guitar is to be kept at home, a hard one if it is going to be moved around, or the toddler can get access to it.

A soft, lint free duster can give the guitar a once over after it is played, removing finger marks, and specialist cleaners can be used to make it sparkle.

When the guitar is not in use, store it in a dry room, out of direct sunlight, away from a radiator and in a moderate temperature. Properly looked after, a guitar will last for life. In fact, for generations.

Buying a Guitar

Some things better with age. Cheese, fine red wine, Jane Fonda…many musical instruments also fit into this category. The guitar is no different. As the wood matures and settles, so the sound improves in quality. Therefore, there is no real need to buy new when $50 at a second hand will get a decent and very usable model. Double that for a new one.

But whether buying new or second hand, try out the instrument. Check that its weight is comfortable, and it is the right size. Elvis Presley played on a ¾ size instrument through the early part of his career, but he was a little special. Basically, make sure the guitar feels right when you hold it.

Check for cracks anywhere – if you find one walk away; a guitar is an instrument designed to take the stresses of tight strings, if there is a fault, it won't last for long. Check that there is no bowing on the back, and that the neck is straight.

Surface damage such as light scratches won't matter if they have not damaged the wood but if there are buzzes when played and the cause is not obvious (such as too much overhanging string at the head) then look elsewhere.

Make sure that the bridge is secure and the tuning parts are all in good condition.

Playing Lead

The lead guitarist is the quarter back, the centre forward, the Ferrari, the Tom Cruise of the guitar world. In other words, the glamour player. Listen to Pink Floyd or Dire Straits or Eric Clapton and hear the astonishing lead guitar melodies and riffs that take the music to that ultimate destination. Of course, just as Mr Cruise needs his support players and the quarterback (his team mates), so the lead is nothing without his rhythm back up.

But if lead is what you want, then a number of skills need to be developed. Some musical knowledge is needed, as lead improvisations come from an understanding of the constituent parts of the chord structure and key signatures being played.

Competency with both hands is needed. The left often picks notes at the end of the neck close to the body, where the frets are narrower, and more precision is needed. At the same time, picking notes with a plectrum is harder than doing it with the fingers.

But, as always, practice makes perfect and that starring role comes to those who want it and work for it.

If it is for you, start by grasping the first position. This is where notes are played using the first four frets, with the index finger on string one, and so forth ending with the little finger on fret four. Once tunes, melodies, harmonies and riffs* can be picked from here, then you can move on to working further down the fret board.

Accessories

Here is a list of some helpful accessories. Not all of these are required, so we have listed a usefulness factor after each. 1/5 means you may not need this item whereas 5/5 means you should have that item for playing regularly.

- *Stand* - frame for holding the guitar when it is not being used. It will add protection to the guitar and help preserve its life.   4/5
- *Footstool* – a handy device for serious Spanish guitar players and beginners as they get the guitar position right. To be honest, though, a pile of books works as well.   1/5

- *Plectrums and Picks* – essentials, especially plectrums, for the acoustic and electric guitar player. 5/5 (plectrums) 2/5 (finger picks)
- *Tuning Paraphernalia* – necessary in the old days, when a tuning fork was the only way to get into tune if there was no piano in the house. Nowadays it is all available online. 3/5 (because an portable tuner is always handy)
- *Metronome* – a handy tool for the beginner. A good, old fashioned metronome does the job and looks great, but as with tuning equipment, a metronome can be found for free through an app or online. 3/5 (but only for its decorative qualities)
- *Guitar Cover* – it will prolong the life of your instrument. 5/5
- *Strap* – depends on the type of guitar. Classical or Spanish guitars rarely come with strap holders as they are meant to be played sitting down. But if you have an electric, then you look a bit silly playing while sitting, at least if there is an audience. 3/5
- *Amplifier* – in the old days, your amp could double as a nuclear fallout shelter, so big and sturdy was the speaker. Now, for $50, a tiny amp capable of filling a large hall with sound is readily available. Pay more, and all kinds of effects will come as well. 5/5 for electric guitars.
- *Effects Pedals* – as spectacular as it looks, stamping on pedals while sweat pours of your face staining the silver lycra and making the Bowie Make Up run, these are a bit, well, seventies. Just get a decent amp. 0/5

- *Music Stand* – from the mad to the sensible. A music stand will hold your music at the right level whether you stand or sit. Admittedly, a table also works, as does a chair and, if your eyesight is good enough, the floor. But, a music stands makes you look professional 2/5

Chapter Ten: Glossary – In Very Simplified Terms

Acoustic Guitar – Steel stringed and slightly larger than a classical guitar. Associated with folk music, some pop music. Ideal for strumming or picking.

Arpeggiated Chord – a chord where the individual notes are picked out one at a time.

Barre – Using the first finger to cover all six strings. This has the effect of allowing the basic chord shape to be played anywhere on the guitar neck. So, for example, the E shape creates the chord E when there is no barre. With a first fret barre, and the same shape after it, the chord moves up from an E to an F, one more and it becomes F#, next G, G#. A, A# (usually called Bb of B flat), C, C#, D, Eb (the same as D#) and then back to E.

Bass Guitar – Not covered in this book, but a four-stringed variety, with each string of a lower pitch than in the six-string variety, usually electric.

Chord – a combination of notes played together.

Classical Guitar – sometimes called Spanish Guitar, these are slightly smaller than other types usually. They are nylon stringed and can be used for classical music, finger picking and, sometimes, strumming.

Clef – the symbol in music which gives an indication of pitch. The guitar uses the treble clef, but never the bass clef. The clef appears at the beginning of a sheet of music.

Electric Guitar – Played through an amp. The easy action of electric guitars makes them comfortable to play. Ideal for lead or rhythm work. Less good for finger picking.

Finger Picking – playing notes individually, occasionally in pairs, with the thumb and fingers of the right (for right handed guitarists) hand.

Finger Style – see Finger Picking

Fret – The zones marked on the neck of the guitar. Each fret is marked by a narrow strip which runs perpendicular to and below the strings.

Fretboard – the frets on the neck of the guitar.

Hammer – playing a note by banging the left hand onto the string at the correct fret for the note.

Harmonics – bell like sounds played by placing the finger of the left hand lightly on the string directly above the fret marker. As the string is plucked, the finger lifts. A good place to practice is on the 12th fret for each string, where harmonics are easy to play.

Hawaiian Guitar – often played flat, they are tuned by using a hollow tube, which creates a unique, smooth and tropical sound. It is possible to buy the tubes and use them on other kinds of guitars.

Jamming, or Jam Session – informal playing with others.

Key – music is written in a 'key' – it tells you the combination of 'rules' that make the piece sound 'right'. The guitar is tuned to the key of E minor 7 with a suspension. There, that makes a lot of sense. It is possible to tune a guitar to a different key, but there are risks; the strings have a limit to which they can be stretched, and will snap if over tightened. Equally, if too slack, they will 'buzz' when played. It is best to stick in the natural key, which is changed through utilizing the frets and different chord placements.

Major Chords – those that sound full and complete.

Minor Chords – those chords that have a kind of questioning quality to them.

Notes – a note is the individual note that is made by playing a string. The notes change when the finger pushes down a string in a fret.

Octave – the group of eight notes between the same notes at different pitches. So, from C to C is an octave where D, E, F, G, A and B all fit between the two C notes.

Open String – this is the string when played with no notes pressed down on the frets. Starting from the string at the TOP of the guitar, the thickest string (which, confusingly, is the lowest note) they are E A D G B E.

Pick – sometimes called a plectrum, this is a triangular piece of thin plastic that comes in different widths – thin or light, medium and thick or heavy. It is used to strike the strings in an upwards or downward motion when strumming.

Plectrum – sometimes called a pick, this is a triangular piece of thin plastic that comes in different widths – thin or light, medium and thick or heavy. It is used to strike the strings in an upwards or downward motion when strumming.

Plucking – the action by which a note or notes are played by the right hand pulling the strings with a plucking action.

Pull off – a note played by the finger of the left hand pulling away from the string with a sharp, plucking action.

Riff – a repeated pattern of notes or chords.

Seventh Chords – a chord with an extra note.

Spanish Guitar - sometimes called Classical Guitar, these are slightly smaller than other types usually. They are nylon stringed and can be used for classical music, finger picking and, sometimes, strumming.

Strumming – the action of striking down the strings either with the thumb or plectrum (occasionally the first finger) when playing a chord.

Timbre – the musical quality of the sound created, often connected to mood and atmosphere.

Tuning or Tuned - these are the individual notes of the open strings. When played open (see above) they produce the following notes (see above). Starting from the string at the TOP of the guitar, the thickest string (which, confusingly, is the lowest note) they are E A D G B E.

Twelve String Guitars – as it suggests, twelve strings with clever tuning, creates a very full sound when strummed. Often used for country or folk type music.

Final Words

You have now reached the end of this introduction to the guitar. You could well be an expert player, about to organize your first gig in front of 1000 people at the local concert hall.

Much more likely is that practice, practice and more practice is what is needed next.

But competence will come quickly, given a bit of time. Twenty minutes a day will help you see rapid improvements in your playing and the acquisition of more and more skills.

Guitar playing is common, so it is easy to find advice from friends or the world wide web when you hit a problem. And that is a part of the joy of playing a guitar, or indeed any musical instrument.

You become a part of a community; a non-competitive, supportive and interesting one. There is enormous pleasure in playing your guitar by yourself, but even more by joining with others in a band, or just a friendly jam session* can be a lot of fun.

Make that your next step and now you are on the road to becoming a musician!

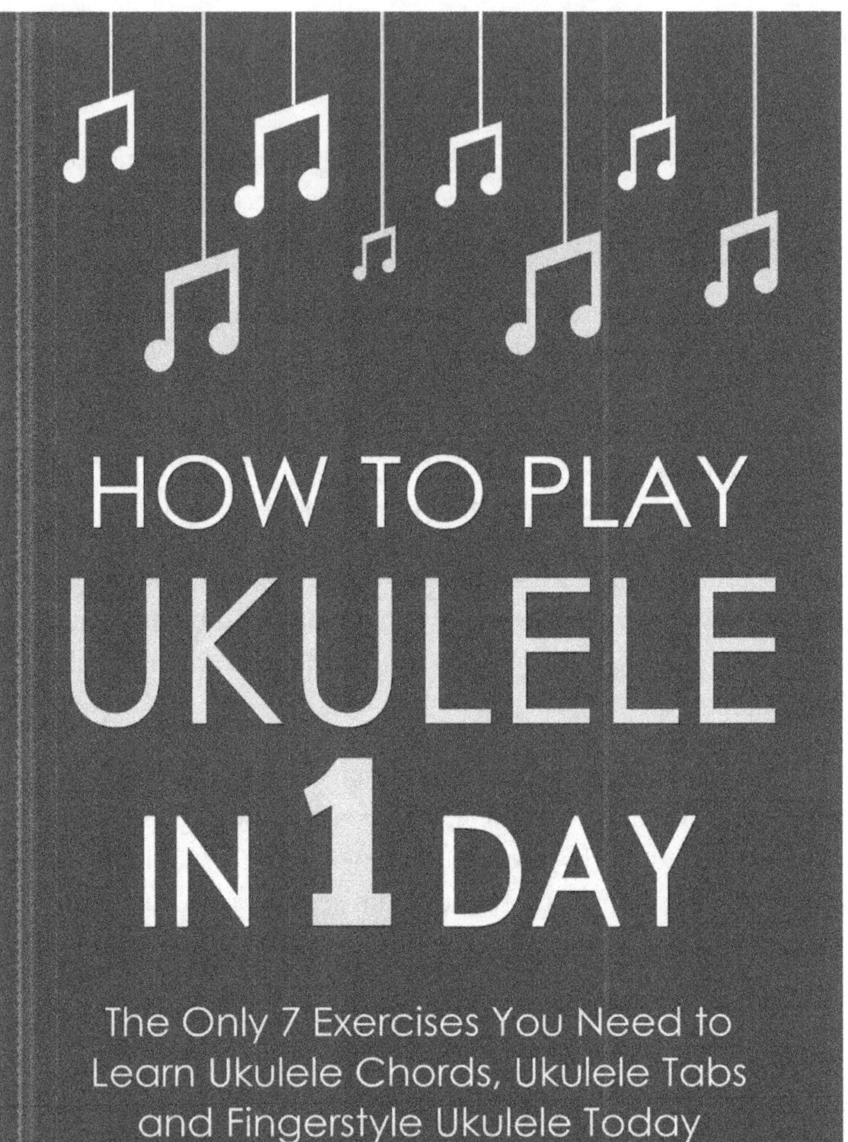

HOW TO PLAY
UKULELE
IN 1 DAY
The Only 7 Exercises You Need to
Learn Ukulele Chords, Ukulele Tabs
and Fingerstyle Ukulele Today
PRESTON HOFFMAN

88

BOOK 2

HOW TO PLAY UKULELE: IN 1 DAY

The Only 7 Exercises You Need to Learn Ukulele Chords, Ukulele Tabs and Fingerstyle Ukulele Today

Preston Hoffman

Table of Contents

Introduction

Welcome to '*How to Play Ukulele In 1 Day - The Only 7 Exercises You Need to Learn Ukulele Chords, Ukulele Tabs and Fingerstyle Ukulele Today*'! Thank you for purchasing my book. And congratulations! You have just taken the first step in learning how to play the ukulele in one day.

Whether you are learning to read music for the first time or are already a pro musician, this book will provide a collection of useful tips in seven easy-to-follow exercises that will get you playing the ukulele in one day.

The seven exercises cover the basic essentials of ukulele playing from how to buy your first ukulele and read chords to learning to fingerpick and strum your favourite songs.

I've been a musician for many years, playing all kinds of instruments from the guitar and piano to the drum and other percussion instruments. However, I've always had a soft spot for the ukulele. I love its cheerful sound and the diversity of music you can produce with it. When I first started playing it, I spent days of trial and error to get everything right. It wasn't easy, and I would have loved a guide on how to play. That's why I decided to gather my experience and research to present a comprehensive guide to playing the ukulele for anyone starting out.

It's an incredible instrument and it is, in fact, not that difficult to play. That's why I created seven easy steps to learn the ukulele in one day, so you can get the same amount of joy that I get playing it.

Enjoy the book! I hope you get as much pleasure out of reading it as I did writing and researching it.

Chapter One: Buying Your Ukulele

In this chapter, we will look at the main points you should consider before buying your ukulele.

Once you decide to start playing the ukulele, it's important that you invest in a good instrument that will produce a good sound and will last a long time. The first step is knowing your different ukuleles. Here are some points you should know.

> Most of the basic music shops will sell the Mahalo. They are a cheap and cheerful type of ukulele and come in every colour imaginable. While they tend to be popular in schools and for beginner ukulele players, they are not the best quality. If you really want to learn the ukulele, it's best to upgrade to something a bit better.

> A good quality ukulele is the Kala which isn't too expensive and produces a much better, clearer sound than the Mahalo. See if your local music retailer has Kalas in stock and test out a couple there. Alternatively, you can search online for a decent ukulele. Make sure you search on reputable music retailer websites to get the best quality ukulele you can and ask musicians that you know or even on online forums to get some recommendations for suppliers.

▸   However, there is more to the ukulele than buying the right brand and type. Another important factor is the strings as these are responsible for producing a good – or bad – sound. Good quality strings are not that expensive and are worth paying extra to ensure your ukulele is in the best quality possible. So, how can you be sure you are getting the best type of strings? Aquila is an excellent brand and will produce a nice, crisp sound. It's best to avoid the ukuleles with plastic-looking strings as these not only can break easily but they tend to produce a poor-quality sound.

▸   There are four sizes of ukulele. These are the soprano, concert, tenor, and baritone. The soprano can be considered the traditional ukulele with its classic ukulele sound and its small size of 20 inches. The next size up is the concert ukulele at 23 inches and is a little bit easier to handle than the soprano. A little bigger at 26 inches with a deeper sound is the tenor and is popular among professional ukulele players. Finally, there is the baritone which is the largest ukulele at 30 inches. This last type is probably the least popular among ukulele players who tend to be drawn towards the small size of the ukulele and, as a result, prefer to use smaller types.

Chapter Summary

In this chapter, you learned some tips on what to look out for when buying your first ukulele and some of the differences between the different types.

- When buying a ukulele, it's best to try and get the highest quality possible to make sure your instrument will last a long time and produce a quality sound.

- There are four different common types of ukulele. The soprano is the smallest and the type most associated with the ukulele. The baritone is the largest and the least popular due to its size.

In the next chapter, we will move onto the first lesson on how to learn the ukulele in one day. The first lesson will look at the different parts of the ukulele and how to hold it.

Chapter Two: Lesson One: The Parts of the Ukulele and How to Hold It

In order to learn how to play the ukulele, you first need to know the main parts of the instrument and how to hold it. In this chapter, we will be looking at the basics to get you started.

Why do I Need to Know the Parts of the Ukulele?

You may be keen to dive straight in and start playing, but first you need to learn the names of the parts. Why? Because this will allow you to tune, restring, and essentially take care of ukulele better. This is essential to produce a good quality sound and to make your instrument last longer.

Let's get familiar with the ukulele. Below is a picture of a ukulele.

It is made up of several parts that are essential for making it work and play music. A the very top, we have two important parts – the headstock and the tuners.

Headstock and Tuners

The headstock is also known as the head and is at the top of the ukulele. It needs to be strong to withstand the tension between the tuners and the strings, so it's often made of wood. The head on cheaper ukuleles will probably be made of plastic. The main role of the headstock is to hold the tuners.

The tuners have one of the most important jobs on the ukulele as they are responsible for tuning the strings. Although their most common name is tuners, they are sometimes known as machine heads, tuning pegs, tuning keys, tuning heads, or pegs. Each ukulele has four tuners and, as they are so important, let's look at them in more detail.

The direction that the tuners point in depends entirely on what ukulele you have. Some may point to the side whereas others may point backwards. It doesn't really matter which direction they point to, it's just something to be aware of. The strings of the ukulele are threaded through each tuner. The tuner, depending on the way it is turned, will either tighten the string or loosen it and this is what affects the sound. On the older ukuleles, the tuners depend on friction to turn it although this is an old-fashioned method nowadays. Modern ukuleles have geared tuners which are far easier to turn and if you buy a ukulele now, it's more than likely to have this type of tuner.

The first rule of tuning your ukulele is to gently unwind the tuner first before winding back up to get the right note. This prevents the string from over-stretching and helps avoid the string breaking in the long run. If your strings are made of metal, this rule is especially important.

Nut

Like the nut of the guitar, the nut of the ukulele is the area between the headstock and fretboard (the fretboard we will look at next) that holds the strings. It is a little ridge with small notches where the strings rest on. It helps to keep the strings in place and evenly spaced out. It also keeps the strings lifted off the board below which is essential for when you want to play the strings by pressing down on them.

Fretboard

The neck of the ukulele is what connects the headstock to the body of the instrument. The surface of the neck at the front is known as the fretboard and is the part beneath the strings. When buying an ukulele, you'll probably notice that a lot of the fretboards are black or dark brown. This is purely for aesthetic reasons and originates from when they used to be made of dark-coloured woods such as ebony.

Frets

Take a look at the fretboard and you will see the strips across it. These little bars ae known as frets. They are lifted off the surface to create a little bump and they get closer together as they get nearer to the sound hole.

Fret Markers

If you have played the guitar before, you may have noticed fret markers as well. These are the white indicators – or dots – that are placed on the fretboard. You may see other shapes or colours, but they are usually white and circular. They are useful to help you move up and down the fretboard and find certain notes.

Neck

If you remember, the fretboard is the surface of the neck and the neck is what supports the fretboard. To facilitate playing, the neck is curved and is usually made of wood to keep it strong and supported. It is directly connected to the head of the ukulele.

Body

The main part of the ukulele is called the body. The shape and size of the body influences the tone as when the strings vibrate, the body amplifies this sound. Ukuleles can have several different shapes and sizes depending on whether it is a more classic or modern type.

The Sound Hole

Like the guitar, the ukulele has a sound hole which, as the name lets on, helps amplify the sound. The sound played will be the loudest over the sound hole whereas higher up the fretboard will have the quietest sounds.

Bridge

The bridge is where the strings are attached, and it is found just under the sound hole. There are two types of bridges. First there is the tie-bar where the strings are threaded through and tied to the bridge. The other is a standard bridge where the string is threaded through a notch at the end of the bridge.

Saddle

The saddle is basically like the nut but at the opposite end of the board. Its role is to lift the strings off the fretboard and works with the nut to keep the strings in place and evenly spread out.

Strings

As we looked at before, it's important to choose your strings carefully. The choice of strings varies depending on the ukulele. For example, on concert and soprano ukuleles, the strings are quite often made of nylon. Other types of ukuleles may have a hybrid of nylon and metal. Some may have just metal strings which tend to produce a full-sounding tone.

Now you know all the parts of the ukulele. The next important part is learning how to hold it. Don't worry, it's pretty easy but you need to get it right from the start as this is what will help you master playing the ukulele in one day. As a note, the instructions below are for right-handed players. If you are left-handed, simply switch it the other way around.

How to Hold the Ukulele

First, prop the body of the ukulele against your chest with the neck supported by your left hand and your right forearm across the body with your strumming finger within easy reach of the strings. If it's a big ukulele, it's totally fine to rest it on one leg whilst your sitting to take the weight off your arms and to stop it from falling.

Your left hand will rest near the near top of the ukulele and keep your thumb behind the neck. It's a good idea to keep your nails short on your fretting hand – that's your left, your right is your strumming hand – as it makes sure that you play with the pad of your finger. Feeling comfortable is key and it may take a little while to get used to holding it in a way that feels natural. Don't worry – this will come.

Chapter Summary

In this chapter, we looked at the basics of the ukulele which are essential to know to get you off to the right start.

- You learnt the different parts of the ukulele including the tuners, the strings, the fretboard, and the bridge.

- You also learnt the best way of holding the ukulele to make sure you stay comfortable and are handling it in the best way to produce the best sound.

In the next chapter, we will look at the chords you should know. This will be the first step to learning how to play.

Chapter Three: Lesson Two: The Chords of The Ukulele

In this chapter, we will look at the chords. They are pretty easy to learn, and will you get you started playing straight away.

As we saw in the last chapter, you hold the neck of the ukulele in your left hand – this is assuming you play right-handed – and you strum with your right hand. In this case, it is your left hand that will form the chords.

To get the chords right, the first thing to know is that the ukulele has four chords. The chord sheets for the ukulele – also known as the Uke chord charts – have four lines, with each line representing one of the four strings.

The order of the chart starts with G, then to C, then to E, and finally to A with G at the left and A on the right. Try to remember them with an acronym, such as, Go Camping Every April, or whatever works best for you!

There are also major chords and minor chords.

>   Major chords – make a definite, complete sound

>   Minor chords – the sound is softer and almost a little moody.

With these four strings known as G, C, E, and A, you can create several different chords. When reading the chord sheets, there are two things to pay attention to. These are the dots at the top of the chart and the dots on the lines. The white dots at the top of the chart means that those strings don't need to be touched. This is known as an open string and you don't need to do anything about them. The black dot on the vertical line indicates which string you need to play and where, by showing if you should play the G, C, E, or A string and on which fret.

As you can see in the image below, to play this note, you would ignore G, C, and E and just play the A string. You would need to hold it down on the first fret, as the black dot shows. If the black dot was further down, for example by the line marked '3', then you would play string A on the third fret. And that's it! It's that simple to read the chord chart.

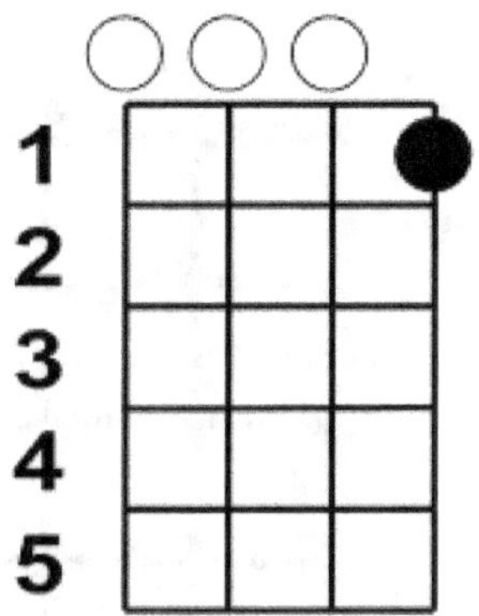

Let's begin with the first and easiest set of chords – the C chords.

C Chords

There are a few types of C chords – the C Major (C), C minor (Cm), and C7. These are the easiest set to play.

The C Major

To create the C major chord, you need to ignore the G, C, and E string and just hold down – or fret – the A string. The black dot for the C chord will always be on the third fret. So, to play the C chord, you need to fret the A string on the third fret.

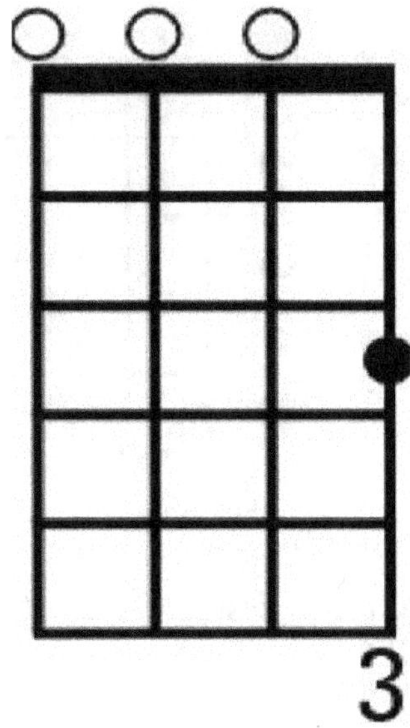

The C Minor

For the C minor, you need to hold down three strings – C, E and A – also on the third fret.

The C7 Chord

For the C7, you need to hold down the A string on the first fret.

The next set of chords we will look at are the A chords. Again, there is A major (A), A minor (Am), and A7.

The A Chords

The A Major

To play the A major, hold the G string on the second fret and the C string on the first fret.

A Minor Chord

Hold the G string on the second fret.

A7 Chord

Hold the C string on the first fret.

The next sets of chords we'll learn are the F, D, and G chords.

F Major Chord (F)

This time, to create the F major, you need to use two fingers. What you will do is ignore the C and A strings and just use the G and E strings. You need to hold down the E string on the first fret and the G string on the second fret. And that's it!

Tip: Using your left hand, place your index finger on the E string and your middle finger on the G string.

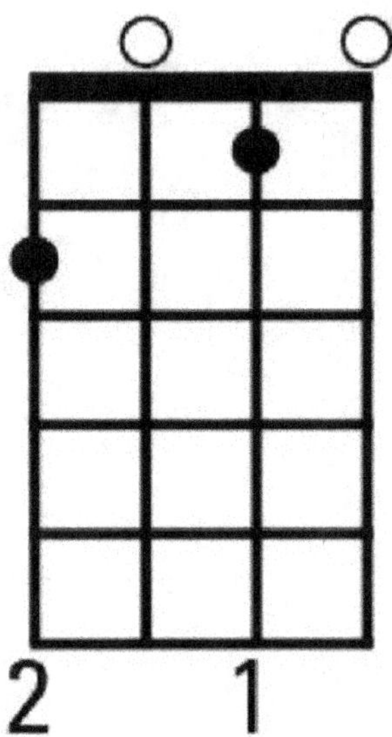

F Minor Chord (Fm)

You need to hold down the G string and the E string on the first fret, and the A string on the third fret.

D Major Chord (D)

You need to hold the G, C, and E string on the second fret.

D Minor Chord (Dm)

Hold down the G and C string on the second fret and the E string on the first fret.

G Major Chord (G)

Hold the C and A string on the second fret and the E string on the third fret.

These are all the most important chords you need to learn in the beginning and they should be easy to learn if you keep alternating between the chords and testing them out until they feel natural. But let's continue by looking at some of the other, slightly trickier chords.

B Chord

The B chord is not used that often in songs but it's worth knowing anyway. It has a complex feature known as the barre chord. The barre chord is when you need to play more than one string at the same time using the same finger.

To play the B chord, hold the G string on the fourth fret, the C string on the third fret, and finally, use your index finger to hold the E and A string together on the second fret. It takes practice but don't worry too much about it for now. You can come back to this chord later.

The B flat chord (Bb) is more common, especially in folk songs. It also has a barre chord.

B Flat

Hold the G string on the third fret, the C string on the second fret, and then you need to play a barre chord on the E and A string on the first fret.

It can be a bit tricky to hold all those strings at once in the beginning, so a good tip is to first master the G7 chord which is similar but a bit easier.

G7 Chord

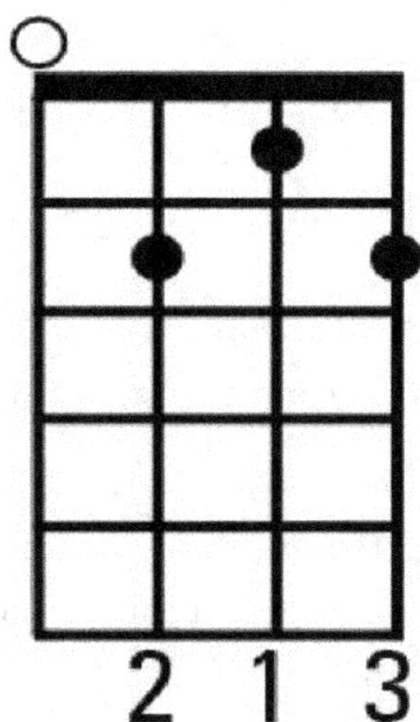

Hold the C chord on the second fret and make a barre chord on the E and A string on the first fret.

Next up is the important E chord. It's a bit more difficult as your fingers will need to stretch a lot which may feel strange in the beginning.

The E Chord

Hold the G string on the first fret, the C string on the fourth fret, and the A string on the second fret.

There is another E chord that you may see. It involves a barre chord on the G, C, and E strings on the fourth fret and holding down the A string on the second fret. Whichever one you choose, learning the E chord is important as it's present in a lot of songs.

Let's look at the other minor chords. These are a little complicated and don't expect to learn them overnight. However, it's fun to test them out anyway for now and learn to master them another day.

B Minor Chord (Bm)

This requires a barre chord on the C, E, and A string on the second fret and holding down the G string on the fourth fret.

E Minor Chord (Em)

Hold the C string on the fourth fret, the E string on the third fret, and the A string on the second fret.

G Minor Chord (Gm)

Hold the C string on the second fret, the E string on the third fret, and the A string on the first fret.

Finally, we have the 7 chords. These are commonly used in blues and jazz and can really add some groove to your music.

B7 Chord

This one is tricky and it's best to know about it now and practice later. You need to use a barre chord on the G, E, and A strings on the second fret and place your finger on the C string on the third fret.

D7 Chord

This one is also a little tricky. Use a barre chord on the G, C and E strings on the second fret and hold the A string on the third fret.

E7 Chord

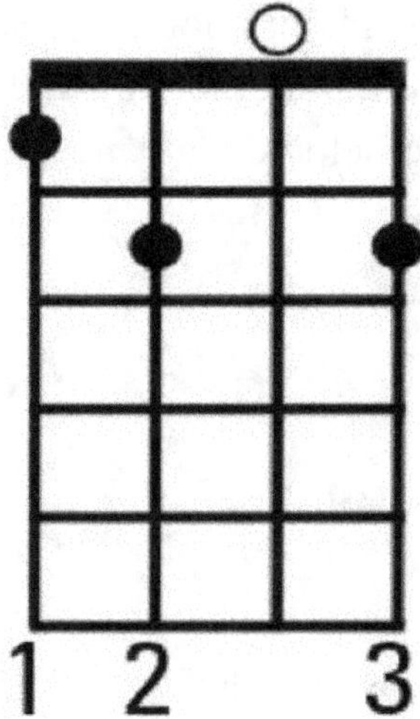

Hold the G string on the first fret, the C string on the second fret, and the A string on the second fret.

F7 Chord

Hold the G string on the second fret, the C string on the third fret, and the E string on the first fret. This is a but tricky in the beginning as it feels your fingers are all over the place! But it will eventually feel more natural.

These are all the chords you need to know in the beginning. Focus on learning the major chords and some of the minors. The chords you can leave for another day at the beginning, but they are worth learning to help you advance onto playing more varied songs quicker.

Chapter Summary

In this chapter, we learned about the different chords of the ukulele.

- The ukulele has four strings – G, C, E, and A.

- The main chords we looked at were the major, the minor, and the 7 chords. Some are easier – such as the C and A chords – than others – such as the E and 7 chords.

- It's worth spending some time practicing each chord individually before trying to transition between the chords. Learn the main chords though and you are good to start playing a wide range of different songs.

In the next chapter, we will learn more about transitioning between chords and chord progression.

Chapter Four: Lesson Three: Chord Transitioning and Chord Progression

In this chapter, we will look at chord transitioning – which is basically just moving from one chord to the next – and chord progression.

The first thing you need to do is to practice memorising the chords from the previous chapter. Don't worry if it doesn't happen overnight – remembering chords can take some time to commit to memory and it is totally fine to keep the chord charts open in front of you. It's better to make sure you are learning everything correctly from the beginning and getting used to where your fingers must go.

Once the chords become more natural, you can start transitioning between the chords.

Chord Transitioning

As mentioned before, chord transitioning is just moving between chords to create a song. Take it slow and steady in the beginning and in time, the flow and pace will quicken.

The easiest step to learning transitioning between the chords is moving between the G chord and the C chord.

To move between them, start with the G chord and place your fingers in the appropriate position. Your ring finger will be on the E string on the third fret. This will then need to be moved over to the A string, also on the third fret. Once it's there, lift the other fingers off the other strings and you are now on the C chord. Practice again a few times before trying to strum each note. It will become smoother and easier with time. That's all it takes to move between the G and C chord.

Next, we will move from the G chord to the F chord.

Put your fingers in the position of a G chord. Then move the index finger to the E string on the first fret and your middle finger to the G string on the second fret. Take the other finger off the other string as you don't need it for the F chord. And that's it!

Keep practising pairs like this to get used to moving between chords. How do you know which are the best chords to practice together though? This is where chord progression can help.

Chord Progression

Chord progression basically shows you the order of chords you need to play. Some chord charts show the chords as letters as we have seen already whereas others show the chords as roman numerals. To keep things simple, we will look at the chords as letters for now.

Music that sounds pleasant to the ear is just a combination of great sounding chords. If you have some experience already playing other musical instruments, you will know that some notes just sound better with some than others. The notes A minor, C major, D minor, and A7 sound nice together, as do A major, D major, and E7. These are some that you can practice together and try making your own tunes.

Here are some easy progressions to start with that will not only get you starting to play some basic songs, but will help you learn the feel of making transitions between chords.

C – F -G

These three chords can be played repeatedly in sequence in major.

Next up is C – Am – F – G

A little more challenging but great practice for getting your fingers used to the movements of the playing the ukulele.

Then try D – G – D -A7

Here are some more easy sequences to practice with:

Am – Dm – Am – E7

Here's one you may recognise from pop tunes.

Dm – A7 – Dm – Gm – A7 – Dm – A7 – Dm

Remember how the minor notes are often softer and quite moody? The sequence above is known as one of the saddest sequences of chords to play on the ukulele. It is used in the song Back to Black by Amy Winehouse, among other songs.

By using these chord progressions, it will help you to get used to changing between chords and start playing some basic tunes. It's the first step towards getting the natural beat of the chords, listening to what sounds good, and becoming more natural with playing.

Chapter Summary

In this chapter, we looked at how to transition between certain chords and how to practice using chord progression.

• An easy beginning is transitioning between the G and C chord then building up from there.

• Some chords naturally sound better together than others and you can make sequences of chords to make a tune. Chord progression is basically the order that you play the chords in. It is good to practice simple sequences in the beginning to get used to changing between chords and to have fun playing your first tunes.

In the next chapter, we will look at how to strum the ukulele.

Chapter Five: Lesson Four: How to Strum the Ukulele

In this chapter, we will look at the art of strumming the ukulele.

There is more to strumming than simply scraping your fingers across the strings over the sound hole. In fact, there is a lot more to it. Luckily, it is not that difficult to learn.

The basic technique is to use your index finger of your right hand with the fingernail facing down. What you are aiming for is to hit the string with your nail as you strum down. When you strum up, you will use the tip of your finger. So, strum down with your nail and strum up with the fleshy tip. It's natural in the beginning to use your whole hand to strum yet you should try just using your wrist to create the movements. This will make sure you don't tire out too quickly.

So now you have the basic technique of strumming, the where to strum part is pretty important too. If you strum too close to the bridge at the bottom, the sound won't be as good and comes out a bit muffled. The best spot can vary from ukulele to ukulele and it takes practice to know what sounds best. However, the best place is usually near to where the neck and the body meet.

To practice this technique, just strum up and down and get used to the rhythm. A great idea for practicing is to put on your favourite music and listen out for the beat. Once you catch it, try moving your hand up and down to match the pace, focusing on keeping the technique right.

Learning to strum shouldn't take too long at all so you will be well on your way to learning to play the ukulele at a strong beginner's level in one day.

Building Your Strumming Skills

The foundations of strumming are the simple up and down technique. Once you have nailed that, you can start experimenting with other tricks and tweaks. For example, you don't always need to just go up and down. You can skip a pattern so that instead of going down-up-down, you try down-up-up by not hitting the strings when you flick your wrist downwards. This helps build up different patterns and rhythms, creating a variety of sounds and beats to allow you to make your own unique music.

Let's look at some other ways you can jazz up your strumming skills.

➤   You can try doing the swing or shuffle strums which is simply when the strum going down is slower than the strum going up. Like the pattern we looked at before where you miss a strum going up or down, the swing strum is simply a way of making the basic up and down strum a bit catchier.

➤   Another way of making the simple up and down strum a bit more exciting is to hit the palm of your hand on the body in between a beat of strumming up and down to get a drum tap as well.

➤   You can also use your fretting hand – your left hand if you are playing right-handed – to influence your strumming. As you strum, it makes the strings of the ukulele vibrate. To create an impact, use your fret hand to hold down the strings at the top to stop the strings making a sound.

Using a Plectrum

There is a bit of a debate about using a plectrum with the ukulele, although it is generally accepted nowadays to use a pick or plectrum.

The ukulele came from Hawaii when instruments left behind by the Portuguese explorers were modified and adjusted to create something distinctly new. In these days, the Hawaiians didn't use picks, simply relying on their hands – in particular, their index finger and thumb – to strum and create music. As a result, the most popular and regular way of playing the ukulele is just with the fingers.

As the ukulele became known worldwide, some people who were used to playing the guitar or other similar instruments, started playing the ukulele with a pick. Nowadays, it is totally fine to use a pick to play the ukulele and some players like to use a mix of both fingers and a plectrum to create a different sound and produce adapted melodies such as rock music.

Some players though, insist that the ukulele can't be played with a pick due to its traditional roots of being played only with the fingers. If you want to follow the older traditions, then playing with the fingers is fine. If you don't mind embracing the modern influences, use a pick too. Some players don't use a pick but grow their fingernails and use that instead! It's all down to personal preference at the end of the day and there is no right or wrong way.

What Kind of Pick?

The type of pick will depend on a couple of factors, one being the size of your ukulele. Th baritone ukulele, for example, uses a long pick that would be tricky to use with smaller ukuleles. Another point to consider is the material of the strings. If the ukulele has nylon strings, a lighter pick will be perfectly fine. Metal strings may need something a little heavier.

How About Using a Guitar Pick with the Ukulele?

A common question when it comes to picks is whether a guitar pick can be used as a ukulele pick. The answer ultimately boils down to personal opinions – some believe that a guitar pick shouldn't be anywhere near a ukulele – but although the size can be a bit different, some guitar picks are fine to use with a ukulele.

A lot of ukulele picks are made from felt or leather so are kinder on the strings. As a guitar pick tends to be harder, there is the worry that it can harm the ukulele strings. However, a harder pick will not cause significantly different damage and strings will always be exposed to general wear and tear and will need replacing eventually anyway. Using a strong fingernail enthusiastically will cause the same damage as a hard guitar pick. This shouldn't be too much of a concern.

An advantage of using a guitar pick is that its allows you to experiment with different sounds and create unique sounding beats. Don't be afraid to test out a guitar pick. You never know, if you really like the sound of it, it can encourage you to produce some fantastic music that is quite unique from anything else!

Will a Pick Damage Your Ukulele?

Not really. If you attack your strings with over-enthusiasm on the pick then you may quicken the rate of general wear and tear. But strings are not built or made for life and eventually you will have to replace them at some point. Using a pick won't have a significant effect on when you need to buy a new set of strings.

So, What's the Conclusion? To Use a Pick or Not?

It's totally up to you. It's worth experimenting with both fingers only and testing out a pick to get an idea for the different sounds. Always remember that you are the musician and you produce your own music so whatever you feel sounds the best, you should stick to. There is no right or wrong way which is why music is so creative.

Overall, a harder pick will help add a bit more volume to your music and protect your fingers a bit. This is especially true if you like playing faster beats. Use a leather or felt pick if you want a softer sound that doesn't produce an after 'clicking' sound that harder picks sometimes make.

As picks generally aren't that expensive, you can buy a few and see which ones you like the most. As you get more experienced, you may find that you lean towards certain picks automatically depending on the sound you want to produce and the music that you are playing.

Chapter Summary

In this chapter, we looked at everything you need to know about strumming.

- The basic technique of strumming is to simply flick the wrist to move the hand up and down over the strings that lie across the sound hole.

- The best place to strum largely depends on your ukulele but generally, the best sound is produced near to where the neck and the body meet.

- You can jazz up basic strumming by missing a strum, using the body to make a percussion sound, or holding the strings on the neck with your fretting hand to get a crisp finish.

- You can use a pick or plectrum if you like. It usually comes down to personal preference.

In the next chapter, we will look at reading tabs.

Chapter Six: Lesson Five: How to Read Tabs

In this chapter, we will look at how to read tabs, an essential skill in learning the ukulele.

The first question is – what is a tab and why do you need to read it?

It's a good question.

A tab is another way of saying music tablature, which is basically a sheet of paper that represents the music that you need to play. It is commonly used among the stringed instruments, such as the ukulele.

The main advantage of a tab is that it isn't that hard to read. It may seem strange in the beginning but it's easy to pick up, especially with practice. It is certainly possible to understand some key parts in one day so that you can start playing some songs on the ukulele almost straight away.

If you have never had formal music training, don't fret. The tab doesn't require it at all. It tells you exactly which string to use to play a certain note and where to play that note on the fretboard. It really makes life easy when it comes to following a particular song.

We will start by reading notes in a tab before later moving onto chords in a tab.

The best way of learning is to see some examples.

```
A ---------------------------------------------
E ---------------------------------------------
C ---------------------------------------------
G ---------------------------------------------
```

This is the general tab table with each horizontal line representing the string of the ukulele and it is labelled accordingly. You may have expected the tab to be the other way around with the top line starting as the G string as when you are playing, the A string is the one that is closest to your body or the floor. If you imagine the head of the ukulele being on the left-hand side of this tab, it can help get some perspective on that.

You will notice on the tab that there are numbers placed on the different strings (or horizontal lines, literally speaking).

```
      A-----2---------------------------------
E-----------0---------------------0-----
C----------------0----------0-----------
G---------------------0----------------
```

The above is purely an example. The number on each string shows which fret number you need to play. So, the above shows we would play the A string on the third fret, then an open E string, then the open C string, then down to the open G string and continue like that.

If that's a bit confusing, let's look at this in more details, in particular, for open notes.

Here is another example.

```
        A------------------------------------
E-------1----------------------------------
C------------------------------------------
G------------------------------------------
```

Here, we can see that there is a '1' on the E string. This means that you need to just play this string on the first fret. So, you would hold the E string on the first fret and pluck that with your finger.

Then, we have this example.

```
        A------------------------------------
E------0----------------------------------
C----------------------------------------
G----------------------------------------
```

To play this, we would play the E string without fretting. In other words, we would pluck the E string without holding it down.

That is how to play the chords when the numbers are scattered across the tab like we saw above – you pluck the strings. Let's look at something a little different now.

Chords in a Tab

Whereas above we saw how to pluck certain strings, we will now see how to read chords presented on the strings.

Let's take a look at the following:

```
A--------0-----------
E--------1-----------
C--------0-----------
G--------2-----------
```

As you can see, we have a vertical line of numbers. This represents a chord. So, you would hold down the E string on the first fret and the G string on the second fret. You would leave the other strings untouched and then strum the strings across the sound hole.

This would give you the F chord.

Let's look at another example, but this time a sequence of chords.

```
A-----2-----3-----0-----0-----3-----2-----
E-----3-----0-----0-----1-----2-----1-----
C-----2-----0-----0-----0-----2-----2-----
G-----0-----0-----2-----2-----2-----0-----
```

This tab shows several chords in a row. In this sequence, we can see that the chords to play are G then C then Am then F then D7 and finally, G7.

This is a really easy way of reading chords and it helps if the chords are written above the vertical lines, as they often are.

The only downside of this style of reading chords is that it is tricky to work out the beat and pace of the song if you don't already know it. The key then is to listen to the song before and get a feel for the beat. Then you can play the chords accordingly.

Sometimes, you may see arrows next to the chords that point up or down. These arrows may be straight or wavy, but they mean the same thing. The arrows simply indicate which way you should strum and it works in a logical order. The arrow pointing up means you should strum up and the arrow pointing down means – you got it – you should strum down.

If you understood all of that, then you are already perfectly capable of reading notes and chords at a great level!

What we will look at now are a couple of slightly more advanced moves. To get the basics of the ukulele in one day, you may not need to utilize the following two concepts immediately, but it's worth knowing what 'hammer-ons' and 'pull-offs' are anyway.

Hammer-Ons

When you come across a tab that looks like this below, it is known as a hammer-on note.


```
        A-----1-------------------
E-----1-------------------
C-----------1h2----------
G-----------------2-----
```


You can notice the 'h' in between the two notes on the third line. This 'h' represents the 'hammer on'. A hammer on is basically when you pluck a note on the ukulele string and then place a finger on a higher fret to produce a higher-sounding note.

You may see the hammer-on being represented by an arch between the notes, but here we see it as a 'h'. In the above example, the C string is played on the first fret and then your other finger will quickly hold down (hammer-on) the second fret to produce two notes while the string is plucked just once.

The next concept is pull-offs.

Pull Offs

Pull offs are the perfect opposite of hammer-ons. This time, you play a note and produce a second note that is lower than the first one. It can either be represented by a 'p' or by arches in between the two notes. When you see arches on a tab, the way to distinguish whether it is a hammer-on or a pull-off is the sequence of numbers. A pull-off will show numbers that go from higher to lower and a hammer-on will show numbers going from lower to higher.

```
      A-----1-------------------
E-----1------------------
C-----------3p2----------
G-------------------2-----
```

Here we can see the pull off is on the third line – the C string. What we would do here is play the C string on the third fret and pull off – or hold down – the same string but on the second fret to produce a note without plucking the string again.

Chapter Summary

In this chapter, we learned about how to read tabs. This is important to be able to play songs and music on the ukulele.

• We first looked at how to play notes where you would pluck the strings rather than strum. The tabs show you which note to play and which fret to play it in. Sometimes, you will see a '0' which represents an open string. This means you don't hold the string down and instead just pluck it openly.

• We then looked at reading chords on the tabs where the vertical line of numbers shows the strings you need to play and the frets you need to use to form a particular chord. It's an easy way to read chords – so long as you remember how the chords are made! You may want to jot down the chord letters at the top of the tab.

• Finally, we look at two slightly more advanced parts of the tab which are hammer-ons and pull-offs.

In the next chapter, we will look at lesson six which is all about fingerstyle or fingerpicking as it is also known as.

Chapter Seven: Lesson Six: Getting the Basics of Fingerstyle

In this chapter, we will look at fingerstyle.

First, what is fingerstyle?

Fingerstyle is a style of playing the ukulele with just your fingers and is known as finger picking. If you are used to strumming, especially guitar players, you may find this a bit unnatural in the beginning but as with anything, with practice, it becomes second nature eventually.

There are two ways to fingerpick when playing the ukulele. There may be variations on these, but these are the two most popular and common ways.

> ➤ One way is to use your thumb, index finger, and your middle finger together. You thumb is in charge of plucking the top two strings – so G and C – then your index finger plucks the next string – the E string – and finally, your middle finger is responsible for plucking the A string.

> ➤ The other way uses an extra finger – the ring finger. So, your thumb plucks the G string, your index plucks the C string, then your middle finger does the E string and your ring finger plucks the A string.

Which one is the best? Neither is better than the other, it depends on what you feel the most comfortable with. You may actually find yourself using both techniques as you become more advanced, especially as some music patterns you may find easier when you use more fingers. Try practicing with styles to get a feel for which one you like the most.

For the sake of keeping things easy, we will stick to the first technique here and just use three fingers.

Let's begin our practise.

Take a look at the tab below.

Here, this tab gives you the opportunity to use all fingers required. The G you play with your thumb – the C string you play with your thumb too but in this case, we will skip the C – then the E string you play with your index finger and finally, the A string you play with your middle finger.

Don't worry about the left, fretting hand for now. Simply focus on the right hand and pluck these notes above the sound hole. So, pluck the G first with the thumb, then pluck the E next with the index finger, and then pluck the A to finish with your middle finger.

Keep doing the same sequence several times until you get the rhythm.

At the moment, you are just playing notes and you get that nice, unfinished sound when you pluck the strings. Next, we will add a chord in the mix. Now you must use your left hand to make the chord and your right hand will pluck the strings. It's interesting to hear how the open string makes a different sound to the chord which sounds more closed and tinny when it's played.

Let's look at the following.

```
        A-------------------------3--------
E----------------0------------------
C-----------------------------------
G--------0--------------------------
```


Here, we've added in the C chord which you play on the A string on the third fret. So, make the C chord with your left hand. Now, pluck the open G string with your thumb, then the open E string with your index finger, and finally, pluck the A string as it is formed in the C chord.

Keep repeating that pattern to get used to the feel.

Let's add in an A chord now.

```
        A-------------------------0---------
E-----------------------------------
C-------------1---------------------
G--------2--------------------------
```


Here, you make the A chord with your left hand by holding the G string on the second fret and the C string on the first fret. Then, you pluck the G string with you thumb, the C string with your thumb again and then pluck the A string on an open string with your middle finger.

Try alternating between the two chords. Play the C chord a couple of times with the open G and E string then play the A chord a couple of times with the open A string to really practice your fingerpicking.

Another easy chord is the F chord. Try fingerpicking several chords instead of strumming to get used to this style of playing.

Here is a short pattern to help you practice. Keep playing this pattern on repeat until you feel you're getting the hang of fingerpicking. A good tip is to keep your hand rested on the body of the ukulele to help keep it steady.

```
A-------3--------------2-------------0---------------2-------
E-----0-----0------3------3-----1-------1--------3------3---
C--0-----------2--------------0-------------2--------------
G------------------------------------------------------------
```

Play this slowly and then challenge yourself to try playing it faster. Remember not to strum but to pluck each string.

Chapter Summary

In this chapter, we looked at the art of fingerstyle to play the ukulele.

- Fingerstyle is a way of playing the ukulele. It depends on plucking the stings to play certain notes or chords rather than strumming.

• Start by practicing fingerpicking notes rather than chords. It will help get you used to using you thumb, index finger, and middle finger for playing.

• Once you are comfortable with fingerpicking notes, move onto chords and keep practicing sequences of chords to get used to it.

In the next chapter, we will look at the final lesson which is practicing everything we have learnt and bringing it all together by playing some simple songs.

Chapter Eight: Lesson Seven: Songs to Play

In this chapter, we will look at some simple songs that you can now play on your ukulele.

Over the last six lessons, you have learnt everything you need to know to play the ukulele in one day. You have learnt all about the chords, how to strum, how to fingerpick, how to read notes, and how to read chords. Now, in the final lesson, we will bring all that together for the grand finale – playing songs with the ukulele. This is probably one of the most satisfying parts of the ukulele, coming second only to creating your own music.

Here are some songs for you to play with the chords and the lyrics. You should recognise some but if not, simply search for them online to find out the tune and play along to the rhythm.

How about we start with a Beatles classic? It may seem a bit complicated but it's actually pretty easy to play. You will feel great after playing this after just one day of learning the ukulele!

The Beatles – Let it Be

For this song you need to know four chords – C, G Am, and
F

The intro starts with: C – G – Am – F – C – G – F – C

Verse

        C   G

When I find myself in times of trouble

    Am   F

Mother Mary comes to me

    C   G   F   C

Speaking words of wisdom, let it be

        C   G

And in my hour of darkness

        Am   F

She is standing right in front of me

    C   G   F   C

Speaking words of wisdom, let it be

Chorus

    Am   G   F   C

Let it be, let it be, let it be, let it be

   Am   G   F   C

Whisper words of wisdom, let it be

Verse

      C   G

And when the broken-hearted people

  Am   F

Living in the world agree

   C   G   F

There will be an answer, let it be

    C   G

For though they may be parted

        Am   F

There is still a chance that they will see

    C   G   F   C

There will be an answer, let it be

Chorus

    Am   G   F   C

Let it be, let it be, let it be, let it be

          Am   G   F C
Yeah there will be an answer, let it be
       Am   G   F   C
Let it be, let it be, let it be, let it be
       Am   G   F   C
Whisper words of wisdom, let it be

F – C – G – F – C – x2

Solo

C – G – Am – F- C- G - F – C – x2

Chorus

         Am   G   F   C
Let it be, let it be, let it be, let it be
       Am   G   F C
Whisper words of wisdom, let it be

Verse

           C   G
And when the night is cloudy
            Am   F
There is still a light that shines in me

          C   G   F C
Shine on until tomorrow, let it be
      C   G
I wake up to the sound of music
     Am   F
Mother Mary comes to me
        C   G   F C
Speaking words of wisdom, let it be

Chorus
        Am   G   F   C
Let it be, let it be, let it be, let it be
         Am   G   F C
Yeah there will be an answer, let it be
         Am   G   F   C
Let it be, let it be, let it be, let it be
       Am   G   F   C
Whisper words of wisdom, let it be

Adele – Someone Like You

The next song is a quite well-known pop song. It's 'Someone Like You' by Adele

Like the Beatles song above, you just need to know G, C, Am, and F chords. Just with four chords, you will be able to play two great songs!

Verse

```
 C          C
```

I heard that you're settled down

```
     Am
```

That you found a girl

```
       F
```

And you're married now

```
 C          C
```

I heard that your dreams came true

```
       Am
```

Guess she gave you things

```
      F
```

I didn't give to you

```
 C            C
```

Old friend why are you so shy

```
        Am
```

It ain't like you to hold back

  F

Or hide from life

  G   Am   F

I hate to turn up out of the blue uninvited but

      F

I couldn't stay away I couldn't fight it

   G

I'd hoped you'd see my face

  Am   F

And that you'd be reminded that for me it isn't over

Chorus

C   G   Am F

Never mind, I'll find someone like you

    C   G   Am F

I wish nothing but the best for you too

    C   G   Am   F

Don't forget me I beg I re-member you said

        C   G   Am   F

Sometimes it lasts in love but sometimes it hurts in-stead

        C   G   Am   F

Sometimes it lasts in love but sometimes it hurts instead, yeah

Verse

C   C

 You'd know how time flies

  Am

Only yesterday

   F

was the time of our lives

   C

We were born and raised

  C

In a summer haze

  Am   F

Bound by the surprise of our glory days

 G   Am   F

I hate to turn up out of the blue uninvited but

F

I couldn't stay away I couldn't fight it

  G

I'd hoped you'd see my face

  Am   F   F

And that you'd be reminded that for me it isn't over

Chorus

```
C           G           Am F
```
Never mind, I'll find someone like you
```
     C          G       Am F
```
I wish nothing but the best for you too
```
     C      G     Am      F
```
Don't forget me I beg I remember you said
```
            C          G           Am    F
```
Sometimes it lasts in love but sometimes it hurts in-stead,
yeah


```
     G
```
Nothing compares no worries or cares
```
Am
```
Regrets and mistakes their memories make
```
F
```
 Who would have known how
```
     Dm   Em      F
```
Bitter-sweet this would taste

Chorus

```
C          G           Am F
```
Never mind I'll find someone like you

          C   G   Am F

I wish nothing but the best for you too

        C   G   Am   F

Don't forget me I beg I re-member you said

          C   G   Am   F

Sometimes it lasts in love but sometimes it hurts in-stead

Chorus

C   G   Am F

Never mind I'll find someone like you

        C   G   Am F

I wish nothing but the best for you too

        C   G   Am   F

Don't forget me I beg I re-member you said

            C   G   Am   F

Sometimes it lasts in love but sometimes it hurts in-stead

              C   G   Am   F

Sometimes it lasts in love but sometimes it hurts in-stead

              C   G   Am   F

Sometimes it lasts in love but sometimes it hurts instead

Leonard Cohen – Hallelujah

This song requires an extra chord compared to the others, so it gives you a bit more of a challenge. For this song, you need to know G, C, F, Am, and Em.

Verse

```
    C                       Am
I've heard there was a secret chord
    C                       Am
That David played, and it pleased the Lord
    F           G           C   G
But you don't really care for music, do you?
```

Chorus

```
    C               F           G
It goes like this, the fourth and the fifth
    Am              F
The minor fall, the major lift
    G               Em      Am
The baffled king composing hallelujah
```

Chorus

    F   Am

Hallelujah, hallelujah

    F   C-G-C-C

Hallelujah, hallelujah

Verse

     C   Am

Your faith was strong, but you needed proof

     C   Am

You saw her bathing on the roof

    F   G   C   G

Her beauty in the moonlight overthrew you

    C

She tied you

    F   G

to a kitchen chair

  Am

She broke your throne

   F

She cut your hair

   G   Em   Am

And from your lips she drew the Hallelujah

Chorus

```
   F          Am
Hallelujah, hallelujah
   F        C-G-C-C
Hallelujah, hallelujah
```

Verse

```
 C                Am
Maybe I've been here before
  C                    Am
I know this room, I've walked this floor
   F        G        C      G
I used to live alone before I knew you
```

Pre-chorus

```
   C                  F     G
I've seen your flag on the marble arch
 Am          F
Love is not a victory march
   G              Em    Am
It's a cold and it's a broken hallelujah
```

Chorus

```
   F          Am
Hallelujah, hallelujah
```

      F   C-G-C-C
Hallelujah, hallelujah

Verse

          C   Am
There was a time you'd let me know

   C   Am
What's real and going on below

        F   G   C   G
But now you never show it to me, do you?

Pre-chorus

         C   F   G
Remember when I moved in with you?

      Am   F
The holy dark was moving too

      G   Em   Am
And every breath we drew was hallelujah

Chorus

        F   Am
Hallelujah, hallelujah

        F   C-G-C-C
Hallelujah, hallelujah

Verse

```
  C                 Am
Maybe there's a God above
   C              Am
And all I ever learned from love
     F          G            C        G
Was how to shoot at someone who outdrew you
```

Pre-chorus

```
    C              F       G
It's not a cry you can hear at night
  Am                   F
It's not somebody who's seen the light
    GE        Em      Am
It's a cold and it's a broken hallelujah
```

Chorus

```
  F          Am
Hallelujah, hallelujah
  F      C-G
Hallelujah, hallelujah
  F          Am
Hallelujah, hallelujah
```

```
  F      C-G-C
```

Hallelujah, hallelujah

Chapter Summary

In this chapter, we looked at three songs that will help you learn to play music on the ukulele in one day.

- We looked at three songs – The Beatles, Let it Be; Adele, Someone Like You; and Leonard Cohen, Hallelujah.

- These songs only need knowledge of five chords so if you learn those, you will quickly be playing the ukulele.

Final Words

Congratulations! You have reached the end of 'How to Play Ukulele: In 1 Day - The Only 7 Exercises You Need to Learn Ukulele Chords, Ukulele Tabs and Fingerstyle Ukulele Today.'

By now, you should have a good foundation of knowledge to be able to play the ukulele and even play a couple of songs. You should be able to read chords and know how to both strum and fingerpick to music.

I hope my book has encouraged you to keep learning and building your skills, so you can become a successful and experienced ukulele player. It's a great instrument – have fun playing it!